For [scribbled out] Thanks for the memory — Chance Massaro

Easy Genius

Awakening Your Whole Brain to Build a More Powerful Memory

by
Chance Massaro and Steve Wallis

We are looking for writers and artists to collaborate on cultural, linguistic, and age-relevant versions of this book. If you would like to join us in this effort… or if you have suggestions on how to improve this book, please email us at: steve@EasyGenius.net

First published by AuthorHouse 09/28/05

ISBN: 1-4208-3156-9 (sc)

Printed in the United States of America
Bloomington, Indiana

This book is printed on acid-free paper.

authorHOUSE

1663 LIBERTY DRIVE
BLOOMINGTON, INDIANA 47403
(800) 839-8640
www.authorhouse.com

Table of Contents

A Most Unusual Book of Self-Discovery

- You will discover how you bring information in and link it with what you already know.

- You will become curious about how you acquire knowledge, skills, and information.

- You will become more intelligent, in more ways, than you ever dreamed possible.

Art by Jerry Hish

www.jerryhish.com

CHAPTER ONE

EASY WAYS TO GET AHEAD OF THE CURVE

Most books are linear: you read from the upper left to the lower right. In THIS book, your eyes bounce around depending on your preferences and your needs.

WHY this strange arrangement?

Different people learn in different ways. What works for one person might not work for another. The science of Neurolinguistic Programming (NLP) tells us that the direction our eyes look affects the way we bring information into our brains. The arrangement in this book breaks the information into chunks so you can read only the chunks that you find most useful. By presenting information in this way, we make it easier for you to read and remember.

In Chapter One, we look at various methods of self-motivation. We were influenced by the works of Abraham Maslow, Diane Barth, Steve Lankton, Stanley Mann, Chance Massaro, Tony Robbins, Napoleon Hill, Ellen Michaoud, Russell Wild, Richard Kirkham, and Cynthia Green. We have also gleaned information from The American Society for Training and Development, Department of Education, and the National Education Association.

What does this mean for you?

If the topic on that page interests you, you might look to other chunks of information on that same page. If that page does not interest you, you can flip to the next page . . . look in the learning stories area . . . and quickly find out if that topic is more interesting to you. You don't need to sort through a bunch of stuff that you don't need to read!

Bottom line: If you learn best through stories, for example, you can look at the same place in every page for the stories about how to improve your memory and your intelligences.

HERE'S HOW TO READ THE EASIEST BOOK IN THE WORLD.

#1 The information in this book is first grouped by subject. Each set of facing pages will address a different subject.

#2 In the upper area, you will find the cognitive and creative information for learning.

In the large central area, you will find the people-oriented information: ways to learn more about yourself, how other people learn, and how to learn in groups.

In the lower area, you will find the solid "how-to" information.

#3 As you read this book, you customize it by reading it the order that works best for you.

Each box is a separate "chunk" of information.

You can read those chunks in any order you like.

WHY LEARN RAPIDLY?

The Need for Fast Learning

The twenty-first century demands super-fast learning. The amount of information we need to ingest and digest is overwhelming. How can we keep up? Most schools focus on teaching information. They do not teach **how** to learn that information for yourself.

Most of us never learned how to learn well. We were told to sit straight, be quiet, be attentive, and then repeat the information back on demand.

Classrooms are run pretty much the same way now as they have been for the past one hundred years. The academic world has largely ignored the massive amount of new research on the brain and learning. The technology of learning has not kept pace with the advancements in cars, computers, or any other area of science or commerce.

This book is all about finding and creating your own system of learning – a system that works for **you.**

The Basics of Superfast Learning

Super-fast learning involves loving yourself and using every spark of your being to live more fully. If you love life, you can use every element of yourself to bring in new information, link that information to a purpose, and use it. Superfast learning means consciously integrating the various aspects of your neurology – how your body is wired, including:

- **Senses: how you see, hear, taste, smell, and feel**
- **Intelligences: how you experience and solve problems**
- **Cognition: how you organize and use what you know**
- **Intention: motivation, what you want to accomplish**
- **Culture: how you were reared and supported by your family and community**
- **Creativity: how you develop new ideas and link them with existing ones**

We start by noticing when we learn quickly and effortlessly. We ask, simply, "Why?" Then we use the answers to learn faster and with more fun next time.

W.I.I.F.Y.?

What's in It (This Book) for You?

Studies show that advanced learning techniques and one-to-one tutoring can double the rate at which students learn and retain information. They also build your intelligence.

This book puts those techniques into your hands. If you apply them rigorously, you can double the rate at which you learn and retain information. Even applying some of these techniques will provide significant and measurable improvements.

If you want to spend less time studying and more time having fun, this is the book for you!

Letting Go and Learning to Renew

We must let go of old ideas and beliefs about what the world was and learn fast to make the world what we want it to be. Letting go involves canceling patterns of thinking that do not give us energy. On a piece of paper, write down the thinking patterns you have that do not nourish you. Burn or bury that part of your past – that paper – to make room for new thoughts to blossom. Focus on a vibrant, healthy future.

Where is Learning Now?

This entire book is about using your creativity.

The sentence above was a test! If reading that sentence started a voice in your head saying that you are not creative, shout it down. We will guide you through information and a series of exercises that will build your creativity to levels you never dreamed. If you want to learn more about the state of education in this country, visit these web sites:

http://www.nea.org/issues/
http://www.ed.gov/
http://www.astd.org/

Arthur's Story

Arthur grew up attending an average public school in a fairly typical suburb. He moved around a lot. He attended grade school, home school, high school, and an alternative high school.

Only in the alternative high school did he learn about his own personal learning style. Teachers there taught him how to more effectively learn for himself. And he loved it. Now he loves having the power and control that comes from knowing himself. He loves having the ability to spend less time studying and more time hanging out with his friends, working on new business ideas or who knows what else.

Knowing himself has given Arthur a lot of inner strength. Now, despite any so-called helpful advice he might receive from parents, friends, or family, he knows that he studies best late at night with some conversational background noise from the television or radio.

What Have We Learned about Learning?

Together, we face a number of issues in education. The first is that demographics drive everything – and you can't do anything to change them. The Baby Boom generation is retiring, and teachers are becoming increasingly scarce. In the business world, senior managers are also retiring and opening up new opportunities and challenges. Our cultural preference for the one best way to learn is crumbling as schools adapt to a stream of immigrants who bring new cultural perspectives into our school system. Many districts are experimenting with methods such as charter schools and vouchers.

By learning in a group, you can take advantage of the learning styles of others . . . and the unique knowledge that your friends and co-workers bring to the group.

Holding On in a Changing World

This book is not arranged sequentially. You don't need to read each page in any particular order from start to finish. If you are aching for action, try this:

Just do it. I bet that you'll find something interesting.

1. Stand up and stretch.
2. Take three deep breaths.
3. Do some quick isometric exercises, pressing your palms together firmly to flex your muscles.
4. Sit down.
5. Flip to a random page in the book.
6. Read only the boxes at the bottom of the pages (the brown ones).
7. Now, do it!

OVERVIEW OF LEARNING

Gather Empowering Beliefs

What you believe is what you receive. There is a wealth of scientific and anecdotal evidence proving that humans get what they expect to get. So, if you want to learn rapidly and well, you can start by telling yourself (over and over and over) that you do learn rapidly and well.

In our decades as educators, we have heard some strange things. Some people actually take time out of their lives to say how bad they are at something. The sad part is that in doing so, they defeat their own ability to learn easily. Let's stop reinforcing belief systems that disempower us!

Here are some simple affirmations that you can say to yourself as you enjoy the stories and exercises in this book.

- I can do that.
- This will be fun.
- This will lead to my success.
- People will help me do this.
- I learn rapidly and well.

Take Three Easy Steps

When they want to learn, your one hundred billion brain cells follow a three-step process.

1. Information comes into the brain through your senses.
2. The information gets linked to things that you already know.
3. When needed, the information comes out in the form of words and action.

To manage this process, you need only key into your senses, intelligences, and personal motivations.

Explore and Use Your Intelligences

You have probably heard of "musical," or "emotional" intelligence. Each of these intelligences is another unique way we figure things out, organize, remember, and use new data or ideas. Every person has many intelligences; we will explore ten intelligences in this book. With each one, we give you the opportunity to find out where your strengths are and how you can use them to bring information in, link it to what you already know, and pull it out again when you need to use it.

The key to improving your use of intelligences is to think about times when you have learned rapidly and well. Next, write down and talk with others about those times; try to figure out exactly why and how you learned so well in those situations compared to others.

In this book, we want to help you explore your inner self so that you can find what feels best for you and consistently use what works best for you.

Tools for Increasing Your Memory

Every tool you use helps you to learn rapidly and well. It might be chewing on a pencil or just feeling the weight of an eraser in your hand as you study. To explore this realm, look into your past and note how common tools have helped you learn rapidly. Then try some new tools.

Keep going; think of more tools and how they have stimulated your genius and memory.

Tools	Techniques
Pens, pencils	Does a specific size or hardness or color work best for you?
Paper	Does doodling help you? How about making diagrams to link key words?

Creative Motivation

If you want to learn something, you will find a way to learn it. Motivation is a golden key with two ends that represent the two major categories of motivators: "away from" and "toward."

To use your away-from motivation, write or say all the bad things that will happen if you don't learn what you intend to learn: you'll feel stuck, you'll be passed over for promotions, your friends will think you're uninteresting, your parent or kids will be ashamed of you. Since you can't get to second base without leaving first, make up one thousand reasons why first base is an awful place.

To use your toward motivation, write or say all the good things that will happen when you learn what you intend to learn. Write that the outcome will make your family proud, your boss pleased, your friends admiring, your pockets filled with money, and your life filled with fun.

Brain Stories

People process information in different ways. If you let them tell you a story, you can quickly get a feel for their cognitive style. Here are the five styles and examples of how they show up in people's stories:

Realistic: "Just the facts, ma'am." This style wants to know what is true or verifiable in its own right. Lynn tells long, and very factual stories.

Pragmatic: "How can I use this?" These thinkers care mostly about how things learned can serve a purpose. Lars tells stories about how he can fix the production line without much planning. But how long does a quick fix last?

Synthetic: "This is like that!" This style involves metaphor, analogy, and connection; how things relate to one another, combine, and create new things. Steve digresses with his stories; everything reminds him of something else.

Analytic: "Take it apart." This style leads us to find the components. Kurt tells stories that start with the big picture and then goes into progressively smaller detail.

Idealistic: "What's next?" The idealist tends to carry an idea to its logical extreme. In one fable, Win Le's wife takes every event to a frightful future conclusion.

When you know how you think, you can use that knowledge to help you learn more easily. In this book, we will read lots of stories about how other people use their modalities, intelligences, and cognition to help find more – and more friendly – ways to learn.

Shape Your Environment

As you enjoy exploring how you have learned in the past, you also shape your learning environment so that it supports you in the future. Here is a preview of some techniques we will explore throughout this book:

Post affirmations on your wall. These will remind you to say: "I can do that," "This will be fun," "This will lead to my success," "I learn rapidly and well," and "People will help me do this."

Post your goals. On a big sheet of paper, in a pleasant, colorful way, write what you are striving for, and post it on your wall.

Keep score. Use a big scorecard on your wall or on your computer. Check it daily.

OWNING MOTIVATION

The Science of Motivation

Abraham Maslow was the first modern theorist to put forth a model of motivation: the hierarchy of needs. From highest to lowest, the levels of motivation are:

1. Self Actualization
2. A sense of power, efficacy
3. Belonging to a social group
4. Safety, security
5. Basic survival

Maslow postulated that we will seek the highest possible level of accomplishment, but in most cases we would not seek a higher level if a lower level were not fulfilled. Frederick Herzberg agreed with Maslow and also suggested that once a lower need was met, it no longer motivated a person.

Characteristics of the Motivated Person

When we are motivated we

1. focus on one thing with our whole being
2. are not easily distracted
3. attract others to our cause
4. find it easy to justify to others what we're doing
5. create the time to do what works
6. lose track of time
7. feel excited
8. feel disappointed when we have to stop working
9. can easily discount criticism and/or risks
10. have no problem asking for help
11. love to tell people what we are up to
12. feel great with every step, no matter how hard
13. are happy and confident

What Motivates You?

Look at Maslow's hierarchy above as you think about the activities of your life. Is your work about survival, or is it a path to self-actualization? What about your hobbies, relationships, or chores? Ask yourself, what are your most cherished goals and what motivates you to achieve them?

Remember: if you don't motivate you, someone else will.

Use These Tools and Techniques to Increase Your Motivation

Tools	Techniques
Certificates, prizes	Find ways to celebrate anytime you reach a goal.
Witnesses	Announce your accomplishment to another person (cheer leader).
Scorecards	Keep track of every effort and result.
List of benefits	Write all the reasons for doing something.
Lists of detriments	List all the bad things that will happen if you don't follow through with your plan.
Approval lists	List all the people you can imagine (alive, dead, or fictional) who might approve of your actions.
Fun lists	List all the reasons why doing what you want would be fun. The more of these you use, the more likely you are to achieve YOUR goals.

Being Creative with Motivation

Setting goals is all about creativity. Imagine where you want to be and imagine the steps you need to get there. Is something holding you back? Some inhibiting habit or distraction? Remember back to how that thing became a problem. Then imagine that it happened in a different way – a way that works out well for you.

Day Dreaming by Diane F. Barth, Viking Press, 1997
Practical Magic by Steve Lankton, Meta Publications, 1980
Triggers by Stanley Mann, Prentice Hall, 1987
http://www.ida.net/users/rdk/goals/chapter2.html

A Motivating Story

Diane hated her job as a 911 dispatcher. She also hated her burned-out co-workers and was a stranger to her children and her husband. What she did notice, however, was that she fit right in with the cast of resentful, unhappy women who fielded the 911 calls. "Wait a second!" she screamed to herself, "I will not live the life I see around me!" A lieutenant came in asking for a volunteer to create a Public Service Announcement (PSA) about 911 calls. Diane volunteered. What could she lose?

Diane's PSA was a success. She decided to volunteer for more things. She organized a potluck picnic and then an awards banquet. In 1999, Diane was recognized by the board of supervisors as a sheriff's department champion. When the position opened up for a new supervisor of the communications division, she applied and got the job. After more volunteering and more promotions, Diane is now a lieutenant in charge of the communications division. She works 36 hours a week on a flexible schedule. She ferries her ten year old to soccer and her six year old to band. She also has a date alone with her husband once a week. Diane has never been happier. She realizes that if she hadn't hated her co-workers so much in 1998, she probably would have ended up stuck and hating others as much as she hated herself.

Get Together to Get Motivated

Since motivation is a combination of psychological and social factors, talking about it with friends can be of enormous value. Your motivational factors are likely to spark others, and theirs will spark yours. Try some of these:

Interview your friends; ask questions about how they get themselves moving.

Ask how other people's reasons for doing something compare with your own. Try other reasons on for size, just as you would a new shirt. Do they fit?

Create a mastermind alliance. Gather with your colleagues and have everybody share his or her goals and plans. Meet weekly to compare progress and learnings. Always discuss the inner voices that helped you act.

Complete These Sentences to Kick-start Your Motivation

I want to learn this information because _____.
If I don't learn this I will experience _____.
If I do learn this people will think _____ about me.
When I learn this I will be able to _____.
When I learn this, my life will be _____.
When I learn this I can stop worrying about _____.
When I learn this I can forget about_____.

I BELIEVE!

The Science of Belief

It's in the Bible. It's in the Qu'ran. It's in the Upanishads. It's in the book of Mormon. It's in the Shinto texts. It is even in modern textbooks. Physicists say that we find what we are looking for. Or that all perception is projection – we see what we believe.

Psychologically, beliefs can be installed very quickly. If someone is helpful, you believe that they are nice. Research shows that smiling will help you feel happier. Sociologically speaking, if everyone says that it is bad luck to walk under a ladder, you will tend to avoid ladders. Knowing that it is possible to shape our own beliefs is a very powerful tool for self-development.

Assessing Your Learning Beliefs

To determine the influence of your current belief system, complete these sentences. For each sentence, write three adjectives that are true for you about the subject of the sentence.

Example: Babies are cute, cuddly, noisy.

Learning for me is _____, _____, _____.
Reading for me is _____, _____, _____.
Listening for me is _____, _____, _____.
Trying new ways to learn is _____, _____, _____.
Asking questions is _____, _____, _____.
Learning with other people is _____, _____, _____.
Moving while I learn is _____, _____, _____.
Applying what I learn is _____, _____, _____.
Being creative in my learning is _____, _____, _____.

Circle all the adjectives you wrote that make you feel good.

Count all the positive adjectives you circled.

7 + = Your belief system is average in relation to learning well.
14 + = You have a clearly empowering belief system regarding learning.
21 + = Your belief system regarding learning is very strong.

To empower your beliefs, cross out the negative adjectives and write positive ones in their places. When you talk to yourself or other people about learning something, use the positive words to help improve your beliefs.

Build the Beliefs You Choose

Tools	Techniques
Good friends	Ask your friends to notice when you learn and to compliment you about it.
Autosuggestion	Repeat to yourself, "This will be fun and effective," before every learning session.
Writing	Write a single, specific, positive sentence about your learning fifteen times a day. For example, I might write: "I, Chance Massaro, will become a spreadsheet expert because I will learn ten new facts each day."

Be Creative with Your Beliefs

What beliefs do you have about your ability to learn?

What beliefs do you have about your future?

How will your ability to learn affect your future?

List here the beliefs you should have if you want to easily attain your most optimistic future:

_____

_____

_____

For ideas, read:

Awaken The Giant Within by Anthony Robbins, Fireside, 1993

Creative Visualizations by Shakti Gawain, New World Library, 1983

Think and Grow Rich by Napoleon Hill, Fawcett Books, 1937

Boost Your Brain Power by Ellen Michaud & Russell Wild, Rodale Press, 1991

The Story of Chance's Life

Until the age of three, I was raised by a single mother. Mom's modus operandi could be captured in the phrase "service to others." Even at that very young age, I saw many examples of her helping other people. Because of this early imprinting, it's really easy for me to think of others and what I may do for them. As a consultant and trainer, I am successful because I consistently help people believe in their own ability and self-worth.

People often hire me because things are not working well in their organization. When I first meet them, I listen for indications of their strengths; everyone has many strengths. I then give those signs back to them by saying, essentially, "You are strong (or creative or caring – whatever is true) and you can do this." People believe me and consistently go on to improve their lives.

Believing With Others

Note places in your day-to-day life where people ritualize a positive belief system. What do you say to each other before a big game? What are the standard opening ceremonies of a classroom? A courtroom? The ritual ceremonies at these events signify that particular actions will follow – and those actions will produce positive results.

You can tap into this powerful force. All you need to do is create some simple rituals – perhaps just be a few words – to use every time you and your friends sit down to study or take a test. By the time these rituals become a habit you will have amazing results.

A Simple Repetitive Exercise

In case you haven't noticed, it has been our intention to steer you away from repetition as a learning technique. Repetition works; it's just not much fun in most cases. However, since most beliefs are supported from inside and outside by regular and sometimes constant repetition, we offer this simple exercise for you to try. Read the following paragraph aloud three times a day for thirty days.

I am a fast learner. I love to learn. I learn with my eyes and ears and nose and hands and tongue. I learn constantly. I learn with other people. Other people help me learn well. I learn using all my favorite intelligences and ways of thinking. My environment encourages my rapid learning. I can learn anything at any time. I want to learn. I am a fast learner.

KEEPING SCORE

Keep Score of Your Success

The simple scoreboard is a useful tool. Its job is to track your progress toward your goal. Being aware of your progress is a powerful technique; it increases your ability in the present by reviewing the successes of your past. Try it right now by making a list of interesting things that you have learned and how you learned them. As you practice your memory and imagination, you will reactivate old skills that you still have at your disposal. You will also learn how you learn.

The Science of Scoring

Scoreboards are also powerful because they allow your brain to unify behind the creative element (what will be on the scoreboard in the future) even as it focuses on an abstract number (what is already on the scoreboard). Scoreboards are used in sports, time, weather, selling, driving, and fundraising campaigns. When you use a scoreboard to measure your learning progress, you will notice that your interest and commitment increase. You will also have clear evidence that a particular technique actually works for you.

What Counts for a Scorekeeper

You can be an excellent scorekeeper if you find yourself doing any of the following.

1. Know how many miles per gallon your car gets.
2. Know how many calories there are in a Hershey's kiss (or anything else).
3. Change your oil every 3000 miles.
4. Keep track of rainfall, wind speed, or temperature.
5. Talk about events using numbers (We drove eighty miles; I have twelve rose plants; our town has six movie theatres).
6. Recite game scores or athletes' statistics.
7. Find a simple pleasure in counting things.
8. Ask for numerical details (How many people were at the party?).
9. Tell people how much something cost.
10. Budget money well.
11. Plan for your financial future.
12. Remember birthdays and anniversaries.

Quick Tricks to Help You Measure Up

Tools	Techniques
Your body	Measure pounds, inches, hair, and wrinkles. Use temporary tattoos to keep track of learning progress.
Calendar	Every day you learn something new, write it on the calendar. Whenever you try a new technique, indicate that on the calendar. Use stickers or drawings for variety.
Spreadsheet	Keep track of ideas, concepts, skills learned in an orderly table (what and when and how).
Thermometer	Draw a thermometer as fund-raisers do; color in the percentage of a thing learned. When you reach the top, you are 100 percent ready for the test.
Coins in a jar	Put a quarter in a jar for every concept you learn or for every new learning trick you try.
Flowers	Create a victory garden by planting one flower for every new concept you actually use.

What To Measure	1	2	3	...	31
Time Studying					
Pages Read					
Meetings					
Problems Worked					
Classes Attended					
New Learning Technique Used					
Learnings Used In The Real World					

Hello Creative Types

We can create something more interesting than a traditional, rectangular scoreboard. Can you imagine how a circular scoreboard might look? The Mayans did it. Why use simple numbers and letters to reflect your score? What about pictures and symbols and more? Let your imagination run wild. Reinvent the scoreboard in a way that will work best for you.

Margaret's Story

Margaret, the director of a social service agency, was desperate. Absenteeism was high, grievances were mounting, errors were rampant, and no one was talking about improvement.

I asked her to name the one thing she would most like to change, and she said, "Morale. If we had higher morale, employees would be more willing to work on the other problems." When I asked how she would measure morale, she said, "Smiles." My suggestion was that we place a big scoreboard on the wall. We asked all the employees to keep track of the number of smiles they saw and give their totals to the receptionist at the end of the day. The results were listed on the scoreboard.

The first three days were awful: about one-half smile per employee. Then Margaret came to work in a garish wig and acted perfectly normally. No one mentioned the wig, but smiles were up 100 percent. Then the receptionist wore way-too-much lipstick that was way-too-red. Employees made jokes about her sobriety and her personal relationships. Result: smiles were up another 200 percent. On the sixth day, four employees wore cowboy hats and used cowboy language all day long. People began to conspire to see how they could reach five hundred smiles in one day. It took only three more days. The place was full of weird hats, baby pictures, Internet jokes, and funny accents. After two weeks, the employees formed a High Morale Action Team ("The Clowns"). This team designed activities to keep people smiling. They instituted dress-down days and dress-up days, one-color days, and more. A year later, absenteeism was near zero, grievances were nonexistent, and errors were down by 83 percent.

Scorekeeping With Friends

List all the ways you've seen games scored. You can use all of these methods with your friends. Create teams and compete for tournaments and prizes. Here are some things you can score:

1. Number of new techniques used
2. Speed of bringing a new learning to use
3. Concepts or processes understood
4. Total pages read

Scorekeeping will keep you focused and fired up.

A Super Simple Exercise

Make a short list of all the things about yourself that you think are cool, or special, or fun. Then, add one or two learning skills you would like to try for a few days. Keep score for two weeks. Just make a check mark for each skill you used that day.

Quality or Skill	M	T	W	Th	F	S	S	M	T	W	Th	S	S
Polite	✓				✓								
Good Dancer			✓										
Generous	✓	✓			✓								
Use Colored Notes		✓			✓								
Use Study Group			✓	✓	✓								

REMEMBERING

The Science of Memory:

The brain is all about creation, connection, and control. Electrical charges flowing from axons to dendrites create chemical packages in nerve cells. These chemical packages are like little buckets of memory juice. Whenever we want, we can dip into these buckets to access our memories. Cells in the brain and the body are constantly creating new packages and recreating old packages.

Scientific studies affirm what seems to be common sense: if you are extremely busy, don't get enough sleep, are nervous or anxious, your power of memory will fade rapidly. Further, low self-esteem and poor self-image will inhibit memory. Many drugs can influence the memory process. Drugs like seratonin, adrenaline, dopamine, and the endorphin group (created by the body itself) enhance memory. Alcohol, marijuana, nicotine, and cocaine can greatly decrease the ability to remember. Even prescription drugs to reduce blood pressure, eliminate pain, or induce sleep interfere with the memory process. Finally, here are a couple of scientific no-brainers: 1) It is difficult to remember something you have never experienced. 2) It is hard to remember something that has no meaning or significance for you.

How Disciplined is Your Memory?

It is truly a joy to remember fun and satisfying things. Then again, it's really awful to be plagued by negative memories. People whose memory is undisciplined will recall things randomly, pleasant or painful. They may also have trouble remembering specific things when they want to. People with disciplined memories:

1. Believe that they will remember (I never forget a face)
2. Believe that the information they remember is useful
3. Integrate new information using specific techniques (essentially, attaching a "flag" to it) so they can draw it out when they need it
4. Review the information regularly
5. Congratulate themselves when they get it right ("I knew I'd seen your face somewhere").

The Memory Game

Observe how your memory works as you respond to the following questions. What do you think of first, second, and so forth?

- Close your eyes and describe where you are as completely as possible.
- What did you have for breakfast last Sunday?
- What is the nicest thing anyone ever did for you?
- What is the song of a robin? A crow? A swallow?

Tell yourself: "I have a great memory, and it's getting better. I always remember what I want to remember."

Classic Memory Methods

Tools	Techniques
"Pegs"	Design some rhyming pegs to hang facts on. The classic is: one = run, two = shoe, three = tree, four = door, five = hive, six = sticks, seven = heaven, eight = gate, nine = vine, ten = hen. Think of the first thing you want to remember as running toward you, the second is stuck in your shoe, and so forth.
Acronyms	Take the first letter of each thing you want to remember and create a word or phrase that is easy to remember. For example, the colors of the rainbow spell out Roy G. Biv. Try this ASAP.
Telling a story	When you want to remember a spelling or a sequence, use a goofy story. For example, here's a story for the spelling of "arithmetic": A real individual thought he might eat turkey in church.
Associations	Steve's last name is Wallis. To remember his last name, I visualize him scaling a wall. The more outrageous the association, the better you'll remember. (Just don't tell people how you remember their names; it might get too weird.)

Be Creative in Your Pursuit of Remembering

Creativity is about finding new things, meeting new people, and putting old information together in new ways. How many different ways do you already know that have helped you (or others) to remember? Make a list. Once you have the list, create new methods of remembering by combining two or more methods together. For example, if your list includes making rhymes to help you remember and studying with other people, you can combine the two into "making rhymes with others." Try it. Then try out your new learning method.

You can also try <u>Total Memory Workout</u> by Cynthia R. Green, Bantam Books, 1999.

A Story to Remember

I took Psychology 101 with Dr. Lutwick. One day, I was startled when a man pulled a gun on the professor. Dr. Lutwick gave the man his cash and the stranger fled. In the ensuing uproar some students yelled while others cried or sat stunned. Then the thief reentered the room and gave the bills back to the professor. The whole event had been staged for a demonstration of perception and memory. Apologizing, Dr. Lutwick handed out a questionnaire that asked for details of the incident. At our next class, Dr. Lutwick gave us the results. It was amazing. Not only did we all have different memories of when the robbery had taken place, what the man had said, and how much money was exchanged but two people even changed the man's race. Dr. Lutwick and the man then reenacted the robbery. They had practiced extensively, so their presentation was exactly as it had been at the previous class. When we were tested a few weeks later, most of us remembered our high-tension interpretations of the incident and not the calm reenactment. As Dr. Lutwick pointed out, the more emotion that is tied to an event, the more likely it is to be remembered – whether that memory is accurate or not.

Remembering with Others

For many of us, remembering in a group is great fun; for others it is an impediment. You will want to establish for yourself whether working with other people is helpful for you. Here are a few games you can play in a group to make your learning more fun and more successful. We will develop these suggestions more fully in later sections and add lots more. Until then, you might:

1. Play "Jeopardy" with the facts
2. Create tests for each other
3. Create a situation wherein you all use the knowledge together
4. Play "pass the ridiculous story," in which you make the information so weird that it is easy to remember

Here is a "Whole Package" Exercise

1. Decide on a body of knowledge you want to remember.
2. Tell yourself a dozen reasons why you want to remember it well.
3. Imagine yourself remembering perfectly and using that knowledge.
4. Using the following sections of the book, design an enjoyable and personal way to absorb information including your
   - Best modalities (senses) to use (chapter 2)
   - Best intelligences to use (chapter 3)
   - Best cognitive style to use (chapter 4)
5. Follow your plan exactly. Remind yourself that you're having fun.
6. Celebrate.
7. Tell someone how well your whole learning package is working.
8. Use what you have learned.

CHAPTER TWO

MAKING SENSE

The twenty-first century demands Superfast learning. By the time a product is ready for the market, an offshore imitator is copying it, and its developers know it's already obsolete. By the time a company is ready to deliver tomorrow's niche services, those services may no longer be needed. The world is changing at an increasingly rapid rate.

We can succeed in this nanosecond world only by letting go of old ideas and beliefs about what the world is. We can succeed by learning to learn more quickly to keep up with the changes so we can make the world what we want it to be.

"Letting go" involves canceling patterns of thinking that do not give us energy. Rituals of symbolically burning and burying the past can make room for new thoughts to blossom. Clear away those parts of the past that don't nourish you, and focus on a vibrant, healthy future that does.

This chapter involves loving who you are and using every spark of what you are to bring in new information and use it for a purpose to support yourself and those around you.

In Chapter Two, we make sense of information from Lou Russell, Roger Hiestra, Burton Sisco, Ann Barry, Donald Hoffman, Brian Tracy, Carla Hannaford, and Thomas Finger.

OVERVIEW OF CHAPTER TWO

Our five senses can help us learn. By using each sense consciously, we can bring in information more easily. This is Sensero Sam; he will serve to remind us which sense we're working with in each section of this chapter.

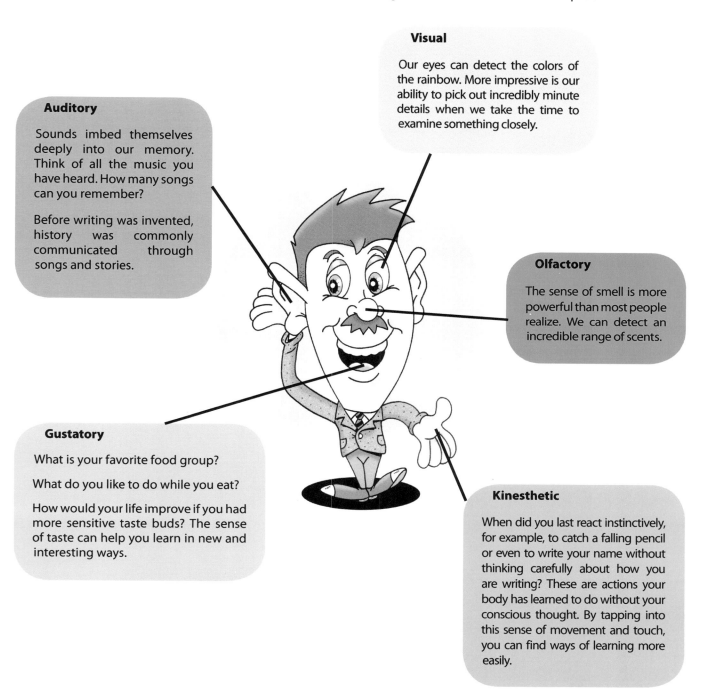

Visual

Our eyes can detect the colors of the rainbow. More impressive is our ability to pick out incredibly minute details when we take the time to examine something closely.

Auditory

Sounds imbed themselves deeply into our memory. Think of all the music you have heard. How many songs can you remember?

Before writing was invented, history was commonly communicated through songs and stories.

Olfactory

The sense of smell is more powerful than most people realize. We can detect an incredible range of scents.

Gustatory

What is your favorite food group?

What do you like to do while you eat?

How would your life improve if you had more sensitive taste buds? The sense of taste can help you learn in new and interesting ways.

Kinesthetic

When did you last react instinctively, for example, to catch a falling pencil or even to write your name without thinking carefully about how you are writing? These are actions your body has learned to do without your conscious thought. By tapping into this sense of movement and touch, you can find ways of learning more easily.

You've used your senses so much, you might not even notice them. Now, get ready to notice them in a whole new way.

SENSE-ATIONAL LEARNING

The Science of Modalities

The learning experts call them modalities. You probably call them senses. They are the five channels through which we experience our world. The ways in which the senses are related to our short- and long-term memories constitute our natural learning modalities. Your modalities are pathways for learning. The modalities that you use best for your learning are your preferred modalities. In this chapter we will give you concrete ways to learn faster by using your modalities consciously. Modality generally refers to hard wiring: how our nervous system brings information in to our minds. The visual modality refers to what we see and the images we remember. Auditory refers to what we hear: how things sound. Kinesthetic refers to knowing through touch or by doing. Olfactory indicates smell (our most acute and least used sense). Gustatory refers to taste. We start by noticing when we learn quickly and effortlessly. We ask, simply, "Why?" Then we use the answers to learn faster and with more fun next time.

Inside Yourself

You'll know you are a visual learner if pictures help you understand ideas and concepts. Visual people tend to think in pictures. They may talk fast and use words such as "picture," "see," "glimpse," "shape," and "looks."

Auditory learners tune in to rhythm, pace, tone, and pitch. They are often musical and speak in more modulated tones.

Kinesthetic learners speak more slowly than others. They feel their way through life and often cannot learn unless they are doing something. They use words such as "I get it" when they understand and "That doesn't fit" when they don't.

Olfactory learners connect easily with long-term memory. You smell fresh-baked bread and suddenly you are back in grandma's kitchen.

Ask Yourself

What senses do you most enjoy using?

How would you benefit by spending less time studying?

Quick Hints for Enhancing Learning

If you're a visual learner, you'll do well to look for and create pictures, charts, maps, and diagrams. Color-in the chapters of your texts. Take notes in different colors. Use collages, painting, and drawing to study. To review, close your eyes and see what you remember.

Auditory learners do well with tape recorders, lectures, and discussion. Playing specific types of music in the background while learning can make it go fast and be fun. Making rhyming or cute-sounding lists will help the auditory learner remember well.

Kinesthetic learners need to move. If you're one, take big notes and always imagine yourself doing something with the material you are learning. If possible, skip the books and lectures, and go directly to the action required to use what you're learning.

Take advantage of your sense of smell by using different spices in various chapters of your text, or carry a fragrant teabag to your next lecture. Peppermint is always good.

Because learning is bringing something into ourselves, eating and the sense of taste can support rapid acquisition of information. Use mints while learning a new program, butterscotch when learning to budget, chocolate when studying new regulations. The key for all of these tips is to create a solid association between your sensory experience and the things you want to remember. You can recreate that sensory experience when you want to recall the information.

Exploring

Many avenues are open to you if you wish to learn more about the senses in learning. You can observe your own learning, you can watch how others learn, you can discuss the process with other people, and you can also explore the information below.

Opportunities for Exploration:

The Accelerated Learning Fieldbook by: Lou Russell, Jossey-Bass, 1999
Individualizing Instruction: Making Learning Personal, Empowering, and Successful by Roger Hiemstra and Burton R. Sisco, Jossey-Bass, 1990
http://www.acceleratedlearningnetwork.com/
http://www.kagancooplearn.com/
http://www.NLP.org

Chance's Learning Story

I learned to drive in just one week because I wanted to get my friends and myself into the woods to collect reptiles. One of my neighbors owned a Porsche and enjoyed impressing me by letting me drive it around the neighborhood. I remember the feeling of shifting the gears. My neighbor, sitting in the passenger's seat, would squirm with pleasure whenever I shifted smoothly. That gear-meshing experience gave me the feeling of what good shifting felt like and was accompanied by my neighbor's immediate affirmation. The Porsche had very responsive steering, so again, through feeling, I learned to be economical in my movements, which my neighbor clearly appreciated.

Here are some logical deductions: I am a kinesthetic learner, motivated by doing things with people. I also respond to both positive and negative feedback.

Learning About Learning with Other Learners

Talk about your past with someone who knows you. Talk about times you have learned something new or remembered useful information. Notice when and how you learned rapidly; cherish those moments. Talk about how you will use what you have learned about learning to learn more next time. Do you know someone who has a great memory? Ask him or her what helps them remember things. Discuss learning and memory methods, and then try them for yourself.

Building Your Learning Strengths

Now we will put our discoveries into direct action. First, prepare. Getting ready to learn quickly involves three ten-second exercises:

1. Breathe easily and take your attention through your body, relaxing all muscles.
2. Allow thoughts about other parts of your life to float away on bubbles.
3. Visualize yourself being successful using what you are about to learn.
- Then haul it in. Using the techniques and tricks you'll learn about involving your senses, move through the material as fast as you possibly can: emphasize speed, not comprehension.
- Now haul it out. Always conclude a learning session (no matter how long) with a brief mental review in which you see yourself successfully using the material you've just learned.
- Finally, note. Make a note of which parts of the process worked well for you and which seemed uncomfortable.

QUESTIONS YOU CAN'T GET WRONG

> **Moving Forward:**
>
> This section jump-starts the learning process by helping you understand how you use your modalities.
>
> Please consider the following questions and write your answers in the space provided.

Go back in your mind to when you were around six years old. Choose a fun or pleasant event that sticks out in your mind:

_____
_____
_____
_____
_____

Describe the event. List the sights, smells, tastes, feelings, sensations, and sounds:

_____
_____
_____
_____

Which senses were strongest?

_____
_____

Go back in your mind to when you were 15 years old. Choose a positive event that was particularly memorable (in a good way).

_____
_____
_____
_____

Write here everything you can remember about that event. Describe sights, smells, tastes, feelings, sensations, and sounds:

_____
_____
_____

Go back in your mind to the first real job you had. Write everything you can remember about learning to do that job. Write down how your senses were stimulated by the training.

_____
_____
_____
_____

Now think of an activity you love to do today (gardening, sports, crafts, discussions, etc.). In what specific ways do you use your five senses in this activity?

_____
_____
_____
_____

Which of your five senses
seemed most effective?

_____
_____
_____

What sense
might have
supported
or improved
what you
were learning
through
another sense?

_____
_____
_____
_____
_____

Did any
sense get
in the
way of
learning?

_____
_____
_____
_____
_____

I want to teach you a very complicated formula for
thinking systemically. We don't have much time, and
when I'm finished teaching you this process you will
use it without hesitation or flaw. Explain here the best
way I should teach you this formula.

_____
_____
_____
_____
_____

What do you
notice about
how you want
me to deliver
information?

_____
_____
_____
_____

Think of all the things you want to learn in the next
twenty years.

_____
_____

Now think ahead
twenty years and
imagine how
you went about
successfully
learning all those
things.

_____
_____
_____

Which senses
did you imagine
yourself
using with
the greatest
success?

_____
_____
_____
_____
_____

I SEE - TURN UP THE LIGHTS TO READ THIS PART

The Science of Sight

The eye is the most complex sensory organ in the human body. The retina contains about 70 million rods and 120 million cones. The cones allow us to see colors while the rods allow us to see in dim light. Despite (or perhaps because of) this complexity, the eyes are easily fooled. Our minds are confused by optical illusions. When we see a movie, we perceive the fast-moving individual frames as a continual image. Perhaps the strangest illusion is when, out of the corner of the eye, we think we see someone or something that we really want to see.

We can use this characteristic to make learning easier. When studying, you can build-in visual cues such as pictures, diagrams, and colors. As you study, your eyes and brain will link what you see to what you learn. In this way, we can use our eyes to fool our brain into remembering more. After all, only 10 percent of sight is in the eyes. The other 90 percent of sight relates to memory. Just think of what you are seeing now, compared to all you have seen through your entire life.

What We See in Visual Learners

An excellent visual learner will:

- Remember sights vividly and create vivid pictures from imagination or memory
- Easily imagine what is on the other side or what is under something that they are observing
- Enjoy visual variety
- May speak rapidly with limited modulation
- May describe visuals in great detail
- Tend to use "sight" words to describe their understanding. For example: "I see," "this doesn't look good," or "I could see doing that"

Looking Around

Look around you right now. What colors do you notice?

Describe the shapes you see around you right now:

Without looking, describe the clothes you are wearing now:

What do you notice about what you have noticed?

Spotlight on Your Visual Memory

If you want to learn more easily and more visually, try these activities.

Tools:	Activities:
Colored pens and pencils	Take notes in different colors, doodle in margins, underline with different colors, color whole pages, color parts of a machine or device, make a flowchart with colors.
Magazines, newspapers	Paste pictures in books, on notes, on machines; put a cartoon sequence on process steps you want to remember.
Marker pens	Color pages to remember them; make flipchart-sized notes, lists, and schematics.
Paper	Use a different color paper for each subject.

See Creativity

Visualization and creativity are clearly linked. See yourself receiving an A+ after you have brilliantly used these techniques. Envision yourself developing some new visual learning techniques on your own.

Look beyond by visiting a laser light show, museum, art show, garden, or by reading:

<u>Visual Intelligence: Perception, Image, and Manipulation in Visual Communication</u> by Ann Marieseward Barry, et al., State University of New York, 1997
<u>Visual Intelligence: How We Create What We See</u> by Donald David Hoffman, W. W. Norton, 2000
<u>Individualizing Instruction: Making Learning Personal, Empowering, and Successful</u> by Roger Hiemstra and Burton R. Sisco, Jossey-Bass, 1990
http://www.mxctc.commnet.edu/clc/survey.htm

A Story You See From Time to Time

Lois was clearly a terrific speller who used her visual learning style purposefully. By drawing a tight outline around a word

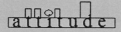

she could remember the word's length (number of letters) and how many of what sizes of letters it had. She would also create a picture of the shape of the word. She visualized "attitude" as a Chicago skyline with the moon rising between two buildings.

Looking With Other Learners

As a group, look at a common item (a dollar bill, a photograph, something on your desk). Take turns noticing things about it; each person must describe something different from what has been noticed before.

Look at how others look at things.

Try looking at the item the way someone else might.

Discuss in your group the benefits of many eyes looking at a single item – and what you have learned from the exercise.

Take a Look at This Exercise

Picture yourself learning a new subject or a new way to learn an old subject. Start by drawing a multicolored flowchart of the steps (this might be the events in history or parts of an algebra problem). Try assigning different shapes to different concepts (e.g., facts are in squares while dates are in circles).

If you can, relate colors in the flowchart to colors of the things you use (e.g., use a blue pencil to match the blue coats of the patriot solders of the revolution).

Then study the sizes of things involved in the job (e.g., the pencil is 7? long; paper is 8 1/2? X 11?).

Draw a freehand, cartoon rendition of the steps in the process.

You can also make a collage representing a perfect outcome for the course of study.

NOW HEAR THIS - READ THIS PART OUT LOUD

Science Talk

When a noise is made, the vibrations travel through the air to our ears. The outer ear shapes and funnels the vibrations. The eardrum then resonates and transfers sound through hairs and bones too tiny to see. These parts translate sound vibrations into impulses traveling through neural pathways to opposite sides of the brain. All these activities give the human hearing apparatus the ability to distinguish and accurately remember at least thirteen separate qualities of sound: direction, distance, tone, pitch, pace, volume, accent, tenor, character, modulation, consonance, dissonance, and emotional quality.

When you want to remember something, link what you are learning to what you already know. As the information goes into your consciousness on a sound, anchor it with a sound you love. Bells, birds, babies, and even someone's voice can be associated in your mind with what you want to remember. To recall information, remember the sounds you linked to the information.

What Resonates for an Auditory Learner

A strongly auditory learner

- ☐ May find the world to be a constant cacophony
- ☐ May find the world to be a constant symphony
- ☐ Loves sound itself
- ☐ Prefers speaking or listening to reading
- ☐ Probably prefers any music to a speech

Auditory learners will remember what they have heard. They accurately recall quotes, rhythms, tones, pace, pitch, and loudness. Other people often find auditory learners pleasant to listen to because they usually speak more slowly than visual learners and they tend to use vocal variety and modulation.

Auditory learners use expressions involving sound to indicate

- ☐ Understanding – "That sounds right."
- ☐ Feeling – "I'm off-key today."
- ☐ Agreement – "I resonate with that."

Let's Hear Your Story

Sounds are all around us.

What sounds do you hear Now?

While you are studying?

When you need to remember something?

When you recall your earliest memory of a sound?

When you recall sounds that make you feel good?

Increasing the Volume of Your Auditory Memory

Tools	Techniques
Tape recorder	Record lectures or your own reading
Noisemakers	Read something you want to remember, and make a unique sound; make the same sound when reviewing the information. Think about that sound when you want to remember.
Drums	Beat out the rhythm of words or phrases to reinforce vocabulary or spelling. For example: "i" before "e" except after "c," or: M-i-s-s-i-s-s-i-p-p-i
Other people	Discuss what you want to learn. Make a list of facts into a song.
Closed eyes	Roll the sounds of the words around in your mind.

New Sounds

How might you use sound and sight together for faster learning and greater recall? Listen to yourself, and try some of your own ideas. Can you think of a better way to explain the information in this book?

Follow these Sounds to Your Future

<u>Accelerated Learning Techniques</u> (cassettes) by Brian Tracy and Colin Rose, Simon & Schuster, 1996
http://bsc.edu/~emoore/THaudial.html
http://www.optimalearning.com/optima.htm

Two Stories that are Good to Hear

Ari was getting C's on her history tests. This confused her because she studied quite a lot. Examining her test performance, she found that she always answered correctly those questions that came from the lecture. Because the lectures didn't cover everything, Ari began to read, carefully underlining parts that sounded important. Then she read the underlined parts into a tape recorder. She would play back the summary to herself while driving or cooking or cleaning. As she listened to her own taped lectures, she heard the information, and the rest of her tests were solid A's.

+

To remember how to use text boxes, I remember the sound of my friend's voice and the whir of his computer. For motivation, I associated the sound with the crowing rooster next door to my house and told myself I had another thing to crow about.

Talking with Others is Terrific for Auditory Learners

Auditory learners are successful in orchestrated group-study sessions and in one-to-one tutorials that click.

For example, while the group discusses the use of a software program, have a tape playing soft music. Stop discussing and have one person stand and summarize the information while the others close their eyes and listen.

To make these opportunities even more powerful, speak with varying volumes, intonations, accents, or rhythms.

How Does This Sound?

Try playing a particular song or piece of music very softly while you study a chapter silently (use the repeat function on your CD player). At the end of each section of the chapter, turn the piece of music up and review the material in your mind. Allow your mind to connect words, phrases, and ideas with the rhythm, melody, and harmony of the music.

Later, to review, play the piece of music and quiz yourself on how much of the section you can remember. Use a different song or piece of music for each chapter.

FEEL IT! – RUB YOUR HANDS TOGETHER AS YOU READ THIS

From the College

Kinesthetic learning involves two basic systems: the neurology of touch and the sense of movement. Touch is, by far, the most complicated of the senses. The other senses have a particular locus (nose, eye, ear, mouth) but touch involves the biggest organ, the skin. Weighing about six pounds and measuring almost two square yards, the skin contains five different kinds of sensing nerves.

1. Chemoreceptors detect chemical agents like capsaicin (the "hot" of hot peppers).
2. Nociceptors detect pain.
3. Thermoreceptors report on changes in temperature.
4. Proprioceptors respond to pressure.
5. Mechanoreceptors register movement in five different ways.

The spinal cord is an extension of our autonomic nervous system; it does "kinesthetic thinking" without our control. We can increase memory by noticing a physical sensation (e. g., warmth, touch, movement) and then mentally linking it with the information we are learning.

Being a Kinesthetic Learner

Kinesthetic learners like to

- Dance
- Play sports
- Build things

Kinesthetics tend to be

- Graceful
- Alive and thoughtful in their movements

They are also slower in their speech partly because language is mostly made up of "head" words and contains comparatively few words that describe the experience of being in a human body. If learning by doing feels right to you, you may well be a kinesthetic learner. Everyone learns through the body; kinesthetic learners do so profoundly.

What Moves You?

What are your favorite sports?

What things do you do best?

How did you get to be so good?

- Friends taught me.
- I read it in a book.
- I invented my own way.
- I learned by doing.

When you are doing something (e.g., work, laundry, driving), what other things do you think about or remember most?

Building a Solid Kinesthetic Memory

Tools	Techniques
Sports equipment	Associate what you want to learn with particular sports or sports moves. The strike, hike, spike of volleyball might become "i before e except after c."
Places to read	Read or think on the floor for one chapter; then read on the edge of a sofa, then at a table, then at a stand-up table. Read five paragraphs leaning against a wall (in four different positions); read different chapters or sections in different rooms.
Open space	Think about your topic while dancing, exercising, doing yoga, and so forth.
Squishy Balls	Study while squishing. Then, squish during tests. The balls are quiet; so you won't bother others.

Exploring

Imagine a movement that you have never done before. Can you do this new movement while learning something totally new? Try it. Tomorrow, check your recall of the new learning by starting with the new motion.

Opportunities for More Exploration:

<u>Smart Moves</u> by Carla Hannaford, Great Ocean, 1995
http://bsc.edu/~emoore/THkinestetic.html

The Story of Jay

At 35, Jay had tried everything to learn to read. He told me of hours spent sitting with tutors and still being unable to decode the printed word. At my office, he cut the letters of his first name out of quarter-inch plywood with a coping saw. They were about twelve inches high. Then we sailed the letters around like Frisbees, hid them in bushes, and used them as stepping-stones. Then we cut out the letters of his middle and last names. Eventually twenty letters were shaped, tossed, and arranged. Jay began to feel how meaning is formed from squiggly black marks. He painted big words on slabs of wood. Because he likes horses, we started with words that had to do with horses. We played "catch" with sentences by tossing words in syntax. Jay reads well today while walking or riding a horse, but he does not read well while sitting still.

Interacting

We often speak of body language as it relates to movements we make that have specific meanings. If I furrow my brow, it can mean I am confused or doubtful; if I smile, I may be happy. Observe your own and other people's movements while they are engaged in learning. This can help us to recognize the body positions that will best prepare the cortex to remember facts. We can open our body and mind to greater learning by placing our own body in the position that works best for us. Similarly, when you want to remember something, you can place your body back into that position to improve your recall. As you attempt to learn something rapidly, take breaks to relax and arrange the body for alert relaxation. Agree with others in your study group that members can describe one another's body movements or postures during a high-intensity learning session.

Building Your Kinesthetic Strengths

1. Choose a complex process that you want to learn. List the phases that make up that process.
2. Review your morning ritual: get up, bathe, dress, eat, gather, and leave.

Now imagine that each phase of your morning ritual was referred to by a different name – a name that relates to a phase of the process you want to remember. For example:

"Get up = Break the equation down to its simplest components."

"Toilet = Delete all redundant terms."

"Dress = Move the terms of the equation into a logical relationship."

Create a new name for each movement within a phase. Use all the textural clues you can: moving sheets; slick soap; slipping arms into blouse or shirt; breakfast texture; the heft of your backpack, purse, or lunch. Each of your physical sensations can be used as a peg to hang a piece of information on. By using those smaller movements to link the facts you want to remember, you've created a daily review process that will enable you to recall information just as easily as falling out of bed.

SWEET SMELL OF SUCCESS - SNIFF THIS PAGE

The Essence of Smell

We can distinguish more smells than we can distinguish colors. We can detect a smell if there are only eight molecules of it in a million molecules of air. Throughout our nasal passages are cilia; they are like tiny hairs bathed in mucus. The cilia capture molecules from the air; the molecules are then bonded chemically to shape-specific sites on the cilia. These send electrical signals to the olfactory bulb, a bundle of nerves about ten centimeters behind the top of the bridge of the nose. From the olfactory bulb, the smells are linked to three main areas:

1. the limbic system (relates smells to emotional feelings)
2. the hypothalamus (controls juices in the stomach as well as the hormonal response of the pituitary gland)
3. the cortex (which will think about a smell and give it a name.)

Although our ability to detect and distinguish smells is huge, we are quite limited in our ability to smell one thing for a long time. The sites on the cilia, once filled, stop sending messages to the olfactory bulb. That's why people have difficulty smelling their own perfume.

On the Scent of an Olfactory Learner

Those of us with a highly developed sense of smell may find ourselves enjoying the process of tasting different coffees or new foods. Below are some attributes of strong olfactory learners. Put a check mark in each box that applies to you.

- ☐ Love a wide range of smells
- ☐ Easily distinguish between similar smells
- ☐ Are the first to smell something burning
- ☐ Easily associate smells with past events
- ☐ Cook "by smell"
- ☐ Use expressions such as "this smells like trouble"
- ☐ Easily recall smells
- ☐ Know how common items such as paper smell

Fragrances from the Past

What smells do you think about?

What do you remember when you smell a pine tree?

What did your grandmother's clothes smell like?

What smells do you associate with learning fun things?

Using Your Sense of Smell to Build Your Olfactory Memory

Tools	Techniques
Incense	Prepare your learning environment with orange to relax, patchouli to uplift and focus, vanilla to create positive feelings, or sandalwood to reduce anxiety.
Spices & herbs	Use basil to enhance brain function and memory, ginger to stimulate and promote positive feelings, and oregano to calm the mind.
Perfumes & soaps	Wash your hands before and after a learning experience; put on perfume or talc before or after learning.
Rotten milk	Associate bad smells with habits you wish to stop or ideas you're ready to let go of.

From the Spice Box

Since the olfactory bulb simultaneously sends messages to three different parts of the brain, you can leverage your sense of smell to create a holistic approach to learning. Think of ways you can learn more by combining smells with physical motion, thinking, or the emotional importance of your learning material. What combined techniques might you develop?

What's Cooking Out There?

The Neurobiology of Taste and Smell, 2nd Edition, Thomas E. Finger, ed., Wiley-Liss, 2000
http://www.senseofsmell.org/sosi/pubresources/reflib.htm
http://bioinformatics.weizmann.ac.il/HORDE/

A Smell-Good Story

Kim already knew he could improve his learning by using the smell of mint. He regularly used mint tea bags in learning situations. When he was unexpectedly promoted to supervisor, he decided to build on his sense of smell to speed up the learning process.

First, Kim selected another supervisor to be his mentor. Kim asked that they meet in the morning when his own shampoo and deodorant smells were strongest. Kim reminded himself to purposefully associate the professional information gained in these face-to-face meetings with the smell of his shampoo and deodorant. In the evening, as he reviewed the information, Kim opened the appropriate containers as he mentally reviewed what he had learned.

When he read books on supervision, Kim would assign a food smell to each book. As he read and later reviewed the material, he would have an apple handy for one book, a lemon for another, and so on.

When he listened to speakers (live or on tape) he would use spice smells to anchor his memory.

Within two months, Kim learned about the people reporting to him as well as the basics of supervision. Ah, the sweet smell of success!

A Savory Mix

Let's say your study group will be learning a complex process. Small groups can be created to do two things: learn a step together and prepare one ingredient of a multi-ingredient dish (e.g., green salad, burritos).

As each small group discusses the step or part (e.g., historical sequence or rules of paragraph construction), they also prepare a part of the dish (e.g., grating cheese or chopping onions or frying chicken strips for fajitas). Meanwhile, the smell of learning pervades the room.

When the groups come together, each small group describes to the large group the part or step they learned along with the smells they experienced. As the dish is consumed, the multiphase process is learned on a deep olfactory level.

This Will Spice Up Your Life

When you get a new book that you will use regularly, spend fifteen minutes skimming the book in front of your spice cabinet. Then, rub a drop of vanilla into the table of contents page to create a positive association with the whole book. Next, sprinkle spices in the pages as you read the bold headers and check out the pictures. Sprinkle anise through chapter one, basil through chapter two, cumin in chapter three, dill in chapter four, and so on.

Repeat to yourself as you do this, "This is chapter eight; it smells like garlic and is about _____." You'll notice that using the book for reference will be a fast process, and remembering the contents of the chapters will be a breeze.

IN GOOD TASTE - CHEW ON A CORNER OF THIS PAGE

The Science of Taste

Particularly shaped molecules of a substance fit into the receptors on the three different kinds of papillae on the tongue. At the base of the papillae (which are visible on your tongue) are hundreds of taste buds (visible only with a microscope). Each taste bud delivers its taste message to fifty or more taste cells, which then send impulses to a gustatory axon. These axons are a direct link to the brain stem. When the impulse reaches the thalamus and hypothalamus (brain stem) we have the experience of taste.

If the substance is interpreted as toxic, a physical reaction (gagging or throwing up) may occur without our thinking about it. If the substance is accepted as edible, the message is sent to the right temporal lobe of the brain's cortex. At the cortex the taste impulse becomes something we can recognize and talk about consciously. Because taste is linked to the brain stem, we can use it consciously to make learning fast. To do this, we must make our gustatory association simple and concise.

Menu

Are you a gustatory learner? Those who learn most by taste will relate to the following:

- I easily recall tastes.
- I remember events by the food I ate then.
- I say things like "tasty" or "chew the fat" often.
- I associate friends with meals.
- I crave certain tastes (e.g., a hot, ripe tomato from the garden).
- I love to talk about food and combining food and drink.
- When I concentrate, I do things with my lips and tongue.

Favorite Foods

When you remember the taste of turkey, what comes to your mind?

What is the best dish you ever tasted?

Do you snack while you study?

What snacks do you like best?

Using Your Good Taste to Make Your Food Help Your Memory

Tools	Techniques
Gum, Lifesavers™	Associate a particular area of learning with the taste of cinnamon gum. Associate another area with Lifesavers™.
Any food you like	Munch popcorn while you listen to a lecture or watch an educational tape. Review in a separate location – still munching. Consume a full meal while reading a single chapter.
Tea	Select a particular kind of tea to be consumed while learning a particular kind of information. Brew three separate cups of tea using one tea bag. Drink the weakest tea very hot at the start of your learning session. Nurse the middle strength warm cup as you study. Finally, gulp down the strongest and coldest cup of tea when you mentally review the material at the end.
Pencils and erasers	Chewing on items associated with studying can help us ritualize and therefore prepare holistically to learn.

New Flavors

Try goofy things like tearing off part of a page and chewing it while you read the page. Opposites can be a blast: imagine sour popcorn or salty coffee – then associate imaginary flavors with what you want to learn. It's all gustatory fun. Make up some to spice up your learning.

What's Cooking Out There?

Taste Experience and Feeding: Development and Learning
by E. Capaldi and T. Powley, American Psychological Association, 1993
http://www.science.wayne.edu/~wpoff/cor/sen/taste.html
http://encarta.msn.com/find/Concise.asp?ti=061DC000

Marty's Recipe for Memory

Marty is an agnostic who was raised in a conservative Jewish home. He observes all of the Jewish holidays. He invites his friends over, performs the rituals, and tells wonderful stories. People always ask Marty how he remembers all the dates and all the names and all the details of the stories. "It's the food!" he replies. Each holiday has its own special meal. Marty loves to shop for, prepare, serve, and eat the special dishes associated with each holiday. Each dish reminds him of names and details.

Eating Together

Eating and drinking are associated with almost all human observances, rituals, religions, and celebrations. Imagine a birthday without cake and ice cream, or communion without the wafer! So use food (or other kinds of oral stimuli) when learning with friends. Just remember to keep the association simple and distinct. My fellow students and I ate a chicken dinner before studying some kinesiology together. We reviewed joints in the human body while rolling chicken cartilage (from the ends of the bones) around in our mouths. We each took a small piece of cartilage into the test to help our gustatory memory. OK, it was a little yucky – but it worked!

Using Your Tastes to Exercise Your Memory

1. Make a list of processes, facts, or relationships you want to learn (see "Sample areas of learning" in the left-hand column of the table below).
2. Imagine what each of these might taste like (see center column below).
3. Next, taste a single thing at intervals while learning each idea, fact, or process.
4. When your learning session is over, taste that single thing as you review the information and before moving on to the next topic and taste.

You can also use your imagination to remember the taste – and so remember the information.

A tasty way to learn!

Sample areas of learning	Possible taste relationship	Things with that taste
Pruning roses	Sharp	Vinegar, habanero peppers
Math	Sour	Lemon, green apple, grape skin
History	Salty	Chips, anchovies, popcorn
Music	Sweet	Honey, sugar, sweet fruit

DESIGN YOUR OWN APPROACH

Use this space to develop a learning plan that moves you away from old and unproductive learning methods and toward new and wonderful Superfast learning techniques.

Refer to previous sections in this chapter to refresh your memory.

First, always imagine success. Next, always imagine that your trials will be enjoyable. Fantasize that people will be interested in your experiments. Use, mix, match, and mismatch all of these modality-based techniques to build your memory and intelligences.

I See

See color; notice all textures visually. Use colors to make charts. Observe negative space or make a collage. What does your learning plan look like? _____
_____

Sweet Smell of Success

Associate bad smells with what you want to forget. Keep special odors in small vials to use when needed. Imagine the smell of the banquet room where you'll be receiving your award. How will you put yourself on the scent of learning?

_____

_____

Make Yourself a Learning Star.

Approach your modality consciously.

Be distinctly relevant or wildly goofy.

Now Hear This

Make your learning into a story, a poem, a rap song, or a ballad. Sing relationships, chant facts, hum a process. Hear complexity, and sound out your troubleshooting. What does your plan sound like?

_____

_____

_____

_____

Feel It

Close your eyes and feel your books, notes, pens, and references. Feel the numbers on a phone keypad and the letters on a keyboard. What if your learning was very heavy or very wet? How will you get a grip on your learning?

_____

_____

In Good Taste

Always tell yourself when learning something new, "I just eat this stuff up." Put spices, mustard, catsup, on your learning materials. How will you serve up your learning?

_____

_____

MORE SPACE TO WORK

(Photocopy this page to create more learning plans)

Remember to link these methods with the self-motivational techniques in Chapter One!

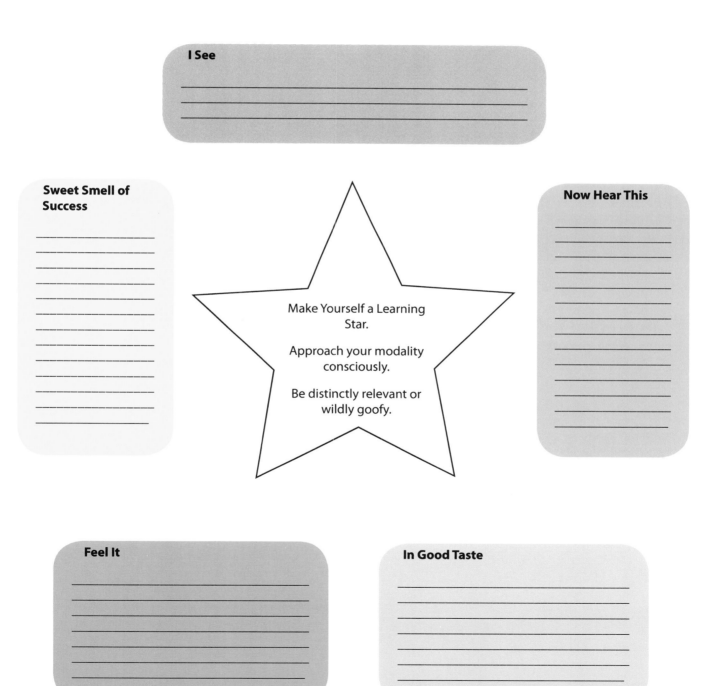

I See

Sweet Smell of Success

Now Hear This

Make Yourself a Learning Star.

Approach your modality consciously.

Be distinctly relevant or wildly goofy.

Feel It

In Good Taste

CHAPTER THREE

TEN KINDS OF GENIUS

To develop this chapter, we intelligently considered a number of sources including Ivan Barzakov, Jean Gibbs, Carla Hannaford, Susan Campbell, Richard Wurman, Roger Van Oech, Sheila Ostrander, Peter Joudry, Edward Tufte, R. Arnheim, Howard Gardner, Robert Horn, Stephen Pinker, Howard Pierce, Julia Cameron, Genie Laborde, Spencer and Michael Kagan, Henry David Thoreau, Steve Wallis, and Win Wenger.

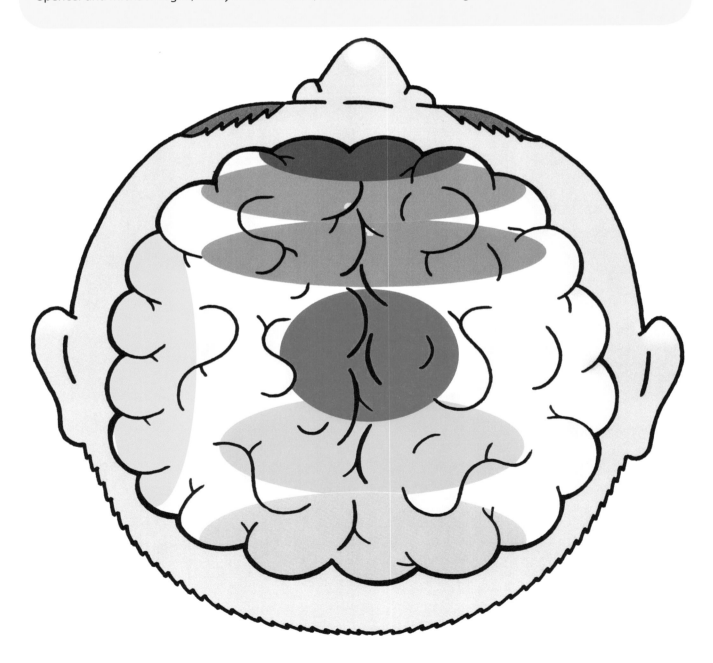

UNDERSTANDING YOUR OWN INTELLIGENCES

Webster's New World Dictionary defines intelligence as "the capacity for learning, reasoning and understanding; aptitude for grasping truths, relationships, facts, meanings etc."

In relation to learning, we add to Webster's by defining intelligence as an acquired skill that people use to bring information in, link it with something meaningful (so it is purposefully remembered), and then bring it back out again as it is needed.

While modalities are neurological preferences we are born with, intelligences are, to a great degree, socially developed. For example, in the 1940's girls were more often praised for successfully completing domestic chores. They were not so frequently praised for understanding and working with spaces outside the home. Indeed, decades ago, when given complex driving directions, a woman might (in an extreme and stereotypical example) totally space out, be overwhelmed, and not understand.

Today, girls are encouraged to participate in sports and to study a wide variety of potential occupations. This social support helps develop their spatial intelligence so that modern women easily understand complex driving instructions.

We can use many forms of intelligence to organize the information that our senses bring to us. We can do this musically, intrapersonally, interpersonally, spatially, logically (which includes mathematically), linguistically, kinesthetically, naturalistically, creatively and existentially. People learn in hundreds of ways to thrive in this world; each area of development from our past and every competency we use in the present can be considered as a separate intelligence.

Our purpose is to acquaint you with the multiple strengths of your many intelligences so that you may use them with increasing effectiveness and joy in learning.

In this chapter, we explore our own mind as a viewer might learn to see and more deeply appreciate the Grand Canyon, the Taj Mahal, Mount Everest, or a beating heart. We will learn about the nature, grandeur, architecture, grace and beauty, art and spirit of how our own mind learns. As we learn about ourselves, we find learning itself becomes easier. With that deeper understanding and easier learning, we can do whatever we want and accomplish what we want. Remember, this is about the fun of living.

TEN INTELLIGENCES

MUSICAL INTELLIGENCE

You love many kinds of music, you need music, and you remember it. You also remember things that are associated with music (e.g., lyrics, musicians). Yours is a blending of right (holistic, artistic) and left (logical, sequential) brains. And you

- Associate music with emotions, activities, or sights

- Are likely to hum, whistle, or sing when you feel good

MATHEMATICAL INTELLIGENCE

You enjoy logical "if–then" thinking and love to figure things out. You feel comfortable with philosophy and science. You are uncomfortable with fuzzy or unsubstantiated thinking. It is logical for you to

- enjoy working with computers or numbers.

- do some math in your head.

INTRAPERSONAL INTELLIGENCE

You know your emotional self. You have an active fantasy or dream life and are sometimes amazed at what quiet time will reveal to you. These descriptions feel right for you.

- I know how I will respond to new emotional experiences.

- I am comfortable being alone.

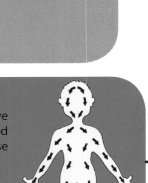

LINGUISTIC INTELLIGENCE

You are interested in language. You like to hear it, speak it, write and read it. You notice word choice and are interested in the finer points of word meanings. The following apply to you.

- I love to write letters, notes, and e-mail.

- I enjoy listening to or reading poetry.

NATURALISTIC INTELLIGENCE

You love nature and understand natural events, patterns, and tendencies. You may have pets, plants, and pictures of nature. It is natural for you to

- Energize yourself by looking at plants and trees.

- Surround yourself with plants or pictures of nature.

Intelligence is more than just the ability to do math problems. This assessment will help you learn which intelligences are your strongest. Circle the ones that seem most appropriate for you.

EXISTENTIAL INTELLIGENCE

You feel connected to something unseen and all pervasive. Your faith gives you strength and motivation. You may connect with these existential thoughts.

- Sometimes I appeal to a higher power.

- Certain music, sights, or sounds feel sacred to me.

CREATIVE INTELLIGENCE

Other people's ideas might not interest you as much –because you are good at coming up with your own ideas. You frequently notice possibilities and options. It may be difficult for you to make decisions because every decision you make is a loss of creative opportunity.

- Does the term "what if" excite you?

- Do you daydream more than others?

INTERPERSONAL INTELLIGENCE

You are really good with other people. You read people accurately and empathize deeply. Sometimes you may wear yourself out helping others. People notice that you

- Enjoy gathering people for parties or events.

- Are aware of other people's expressions.

BODY-KINESTHETIC INTELLIGENCE

You are graceful, strong, and physically competent. You know your body size and your physical capability. You're good with tools and can do complicated things with your fingers. If you want to remember an event, you just move your body the way it moved during the event and bam: you remember. You also

- Learn new sports or dances quickly.

- Are typically aware of your body from head to toe.

VISUAL–SPATIAL INTELLIGENCE

You're good at directions and distances. You can picture a room with the furniture rearranged and may be good at graphic arts. Also, you

- Would rather draw someone a map than give verbal directions.

- Enjoy just looking at shapes (buildings, trees, or objects) for fun.

For another point of view, ask friends or family to read this. Ask them which intelligences they think are your strengths.

INTRAPERSONAL - THE WORLD WITHIN YOU

The Intrapersonal Science

When people talk about near-death experience, they often say that their whole life flashed in front of them. That happens because intense stress makes all of your memories (in electrochemical packages) get delivered at once. This is also why you react strongly to certain things and don't consciously know why. The event has triggered the delivery of specific, related messages deep within your mind. Once an aspect of your intrapersonal intelligence has been brought to the surface, you can metacognate (think about your thinking) and use this process to help you remember purposefully. Once you know how you think, you can trick your subconscious messenger into delivering the information-messages as you need them.

When you employ your intrapersonal intelligence in learning, you dive into a complex world: one you can't really predict. You can use it, however, by paying attention to the nonlinear and unexpected things that arise in your mind. If you're studying chiggers and start to itch, notice that. The itching will help you remember that chiggers actually burrow into your skin and then fall off a few days later. If you're learning a software program, and it makes you think of fish in an aquarium, attend to that, and let the fish continually lead you back to the right command.

My Own Intrapersonal Intelligence

Which attributes of a highly developed intrapersonal intelligence do you have? Circle the ones that apply to you.

- Clarity about what you believe is right and wrong; strong values
- Vivid remembrance of your dreams
- Constant awareness of your emotional state and ease in talking about your emotions
- Enjoyment in being alone
- A strong sense of intuition that you trust frequently
- Trust in yourself and a belief that being trusted by others is highly important

Notice What You Notice

Look around you right now. What colors do you notice?

What popped into your head unexpectedly while you were looking at the colors (memories, ideas, feelings, or impulses)?

You should notice that you notice some things more than others. This is because of the way your past experiences have molded your intrapersonal intelligence.

How to Develop Your Intrapersonal Intelligence

Tools	Activities
Journal	Write your acts, thoughts, and feelings.
Poetry	Read and write to understand your own inner workings.
Songs	Pay close attention to lyrics that are meaningful to you and ask why they are meaningful.
Music	Notice rhythm, harmony, and chord changes; then ask yourself why you noticed some more than others.
Mirror	Look into the mirror and describe your features. Try different expressions, and tell yourself how each feels. Have a conversation with your mirror image.

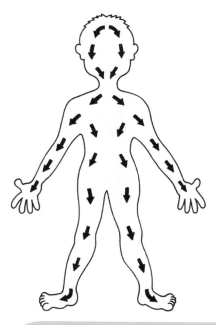

Raise the Titanic

There are many ways to bring the information in your mind to the surface, as long as you don't try too hard. Make it easy and try this game.

First, learn a chunk of information (a sentence, page, or chapter). Then sit back and write down the very first thing that appears in your mind. Next, when reviewing the information, try to first remember the thought that popped into your head. Bingo! You have linked new information with existing knowledge. Also, visit

http://www.usd.edu/thinking/Socioemotional.html
http://www.winwenger.com/overwall.htm

A Story from the Heart

Lafayette is a scientist who has spent twenty years studying how the heart responds to the enzymes produced by the body. Enzymes are chemical triggers that tell the heart how to react to the body's needs, such as by speeding up or slowing down. Lafayette identified six reactions of the heart but found only five enzymes. For over a year, he worked in his lab at Dartmouth to find the sixth enzyme.

One Sunday, Lafayette was on his way to church when he found himself staring at some children in a playground. One child was being pushed on the swing and was going very high. Watching the child yell with joy as she soared higher and higher, Lafayette realized that one of the enzyme molecules he was studying must have a "hinge." Bent in one direction, the enzyme could make the heart react one way; bent in the other direction, it might create an entirely different reaction. The next day Lafayette designed tests to discover if his realization was true. By the end of the week he had proven that a complex molecule could actually change its shape.

In this situation, using analytical skills and focusing on finding the presumed "sixth enzyme" was just getting in the way. Once he relaxed, Lafayette's intrapersonal intelligence could bring the needed information and insight to the surface. Seeing a child pushed on a swing led to a breakthrough in understanding how the human heart can respond to the body's needs.

A Pop-Up Game for the Group

Start with the exercise described in the upper-right-hand box under "Raise the Titanic." Next, bring your notes to a group meeting and share them (don't forget to take the opportunity to review the points you wish to remember at the same time). In most cases, these sessions turn out to be laugh-fests: it is wild to find out what associations other people make to learn new information. It's a free-association free-for-all that makes remembering a memorable event.

Linking Your Learning

Before you study something, create a blank screen in your mind's eye. Gently hold the screen blank for several seconds, and then allow thoughts to wander across it as words, images, sounds, cartoons, or feelings. Take a moment to notice and hold onto anything that seems pleasant or unusual. Write it down, if you need to, to remember it.

Now, get some kind of overview of what you are about to learn. Link what you saw on your screen to a few key words from what you are about to learn. As you read (or hear) what you're learning, bring back the screen image and link the two. It's fun and often funny.

Link again when reviewing. When you are about to use what you've learned, start by remembering your subconscious image; the rest should flow like a stream of consciousness. The entire process should take 10 to 20 minutes.

INTERPERSONAL - JUST BETWEEN US

Who We Are And How We Learn

In some "primitive" cultures, the most horrendous punishment that the tribe can impose on criminals is to take away their status as individuals – to make them non-persons. When the punishment starts, no one in the tribe will look at the criminals, speak with them, or acknowledge their existence in any way. It is widely believed that this punishment will cause the recipients to die.

This book is about using various aspects of our personalities to help us learn more effectively. But what determines our personalities? It is common knowledge that our personalities develop when we are very young. We influence others and others influence us as we grow. Clearly, human contact is extremely important to our existence – and our ability to learn. What comes naturally to you? Introverts can study just fine by themselves while extroverts learn better through human interaction. Your personality type determines the way in which you learn best. Where are you most comfortable?

How "People Smart" Are You?

Mark each sentence that is mostly true for you.

- I enjoy parties.
- I can teach groups effectively.
- I have many acquaintances.
- I'm a good judge of character.
- I work best in a team.
- I am a good coach.
- Most of the time, I care more for others than for myself.
- I prefer being in a chorus to being a soloist.
- I'm happier with people than being alone.
- I love bouncing ideas off other people.
- It's easy for me to listen and empathize.
- I enjoy hearing people tell their stories.
- I feel good when people have fun.

If 5 to 8 of those sentences apply to you, you have a normally developed interpersonal ability. You are interested in other people and skillful at being with them. If more than 8 apply to you, that means your interpersonal intelligence can be used effectively.

Fast, Fun and Sure Ways to Build Your Interpersonal Genius

Tools	Techniques
Pictures of friends	Write learning points on the backs of photos. Associate the learning point with the people in the photos.
Notes from class	Have each member of the study group read his or her notes aloud.
Koosh ball	With four or more people in a circle, ask a question from the group's reading or a lecture and toss the Koosh ball to someone. That person answers the question or quickly tosses the ball to someone else. The receiver must answer the question correctly and then ask the next question.
Flash cards	Four or more players sit around a table with 3x5 index cards. Each person writes a question or a word to be defined; all pass their cards to the person on their right, who writes an answer or definition on the reverse of the card. All players then read both sides of their cards out loud for everyone to hear and check for correctness. Toss all correct cards in the center and write a new card. After four or five rounds, players have a deck of flash cards explaining a lesson completely.

Co-Creating Ideas and Direction

Check out these books and Web sites – together with other people. Then, brainstorm (together) ways that you might best use these ideas.

Tribes: A New Way of Learning and Being Together by Jean Gibbs, Center Source Systems, 2000
Smart Moves by Carla Hannaford, Great Ocean Publishers, 1995
http://braingym.com
http://www.TheGettingRealGame.com

A People-Person

When Ray and his family moved to a new town, Ray was enrolled in a traditional school. The classroom chairs were in straight rows, and the teacher stayed behind a big desk in the front of the room. Ray's performance and enjoyment of school fell drastically. For six months, despite hours of extra homework, a special ed class and even a visit to a psychologist, Ray's schoolwork was mediocre.

Because Ray stayed after school each day, he got to see the janitor. Every day when the janitor came in, he asked what Ray was learning. Soon, they both noticed how animated Ray became and how effective he was when explaining what he had learned. Ray told his parents about it, and the janitor had a talk with Ray's teacher. In his former school, many of the lessons were in the form of cooperative projects. The kids built models and played extended games that had to do with colonial or pueblo life. The teachers blended history and science classes and had the kids teach each other. The kids took tests and did homework alone, but most of the day at school was spent planning and collaborating with the other students. Compared to his old school, Ray's new school stifled his interpersonal intelligence, which was his major learning tool. While Ray's parents searched for another school, Ray set up two study clubs, with teachers as supporters. By the time his folks had located the "right" school, Ray had made some changes at the traditional school and stayed right there.

Interpersonal Learning Exercise

Just sit down and explain a few facts that you are learning to a friend. Then ask questions like these.

- What was most interesting?
- What can you repeat back?
- Tell me something you already know about this subject.
- How might you use this information in the real world?

Do this with three people, and your learning will be solid.

Interpersonal Learning Game

1. Each player reviews the learning material alone.
2. From the material, each player makes up ten questions. These may be multiple choice, true/false, fill in the blank, one-word answers, or whatever works.
3. In a circle, players give their lists of questions to the person on their left. Each player answers the questions on the test just received.
4. When everyone has had a turn, players again pass the tests to the person on their left.
5. Each player then grades the test (it is OK to talk about the questions and answers).
6. When the grading is done, each player again passes the test to the person on his or her left. Now each player writes a few lines about how the particular information might be applied in the real world.
7. Players pass the tests to their left one more time, and each player reads the test aloud, including questions, answers, and real-world applications.
8. At the end of each test, the whole group discusses the usefulness of the questions, the right (or wrong) answers, and the real-world benefits of the real-world applications.

LOGICAL-MATHEMATICAL - WHAT PATTERN DO YOU SEE?

The Science of Scientific Thinking

Logical-Mathematical intelligence is located in a very specific part of the brain above and behind your left ear. The size of this node varies greatly from person to person. It can be an active and productive aspect of a person's makeup or almost nonexistent. When we observe any part of our world and then ask the magical question, "Why?" we turn to our logical-mathematical intelligence to discover a pattern and get an answer. This is the core of scientific thinking. Before 1950,

researchers, including Stern, Cattell, and Binet, advanced theories about intelligence. To these early researchers, logical-mathematical thinking was the only form of intelligence. I.Q. tests focused almost exclusively on discovering patterns, anticipating sequences, and figuring things out. A holdover from this pattern of thinking is the SAT. This test focuses exclusively on logical and linguistic abilities (although it has been known for years that a high score on the SAT does not relate directly to success in college).

Behavior Patterns For Logical-Mathematical Thinkers

Accountants, engineers, programmers, scientists, and judges are typical logical thinkers. These people usually enjoy mental activities that they can do alone. If you are one of these people, you probably find puzzles, math problems, and plans entertaining. Logical thinkers are often able to plan a very complex project totally in their heads. Here's a list of what logical-mathematical thinkers like to do.

Create	Write	Solve
• Checklists	• Letters to the editor	• Social Problems
• Graphs	• Plays	• Puzzles
• Comparisons	• Plans	• Math problems
• Sequences	• Outlines	• Mysteries
• Time-lines	• Analyses	• Mazes
• Patterns	• Computer programs	• Crimes

Systematically Build Your Logical Mind

Tools	Techniques
Puzzles	As a warm up, cut your notes into puzzle shapes and fit them back together. Create a crossword puzzle of key words or concepts.
Time lines	Draw a horizontal line across a page. Label the left end "Start" and the right end "Finish." Write from left to right the steps in a process, dates in a plan, or historical events through time.
Diagram	Draw two circles overlapping by half. Write a date or condition in one circle's free space, write another in the other circle. Where the two circles overlap write the relationship between the two concepts or conditions.
Fishbone	Draw a fish skeleton with four or five "bones" radiating out from the spine. At the tail, describe the beginning of a problem or process; at the head, write the result desired. Along each of the bones write one of the influences that affects the process.
3 X 5 Cards	Write one piece of information on each card. Arrange the information in as many ways as possible (time-order, geographically, alphabetically, or even by which ones you like better than others).

Adding to Your Creativity

While studying a subject, try inventing your own symbol for each concept. You can use your new symbol as you take notes. For example, use arrows for connecting related information, circles for things you know you'll need to review later, and so forth. Here are some books that give additional information on comprehending and enhancing your ability to use your own logical/mathematical intelligence:

Information Anxiety by Richard S. Wurman, Doubleday, 1989
A Kick in the Seat of the Pants by Roger Van Oech, Perennial Library Harper and Row, 1986

A Logical Story

Every year Bob comes to the Burning Man Festival with a different kind of conveyance. Three years ago it was a giant ant powered by an electric motor. The six legs worked in coordination to carry two people. Last year he brought a loveseat swinging on the axel of two ten-foot wheels. This year Bob brought a complete bedroom and kitchen beneath a canopy of solar cells. The room was completely outfitted with stereo, lights, running water, stove, sink, and, yes, even a port-a-potty. When I asked Bob if he was interested in selling the plans to his various inventions, he looked at me quizzically and said, "What plans?" In the amazing conversation that followed, Bob explained that he reads constantly about electrical components, metals, and physical principles. When he gets an idea, like the loveseat suspended on an axel, he just sits in a comfortable chair and plans every tiny detail in his head. Bob wins the prize for the most fully developed logical-mathematical mind.

Being Reasonable Together

Play this game with two or more people. Start with something large, and take turns breaking it down into smaller and smaller parts. For example, I say, "Civil War," and you say, "Causes." I say, "Economics," and you say, "Agriculture." I say, "The North had rocky mountains, which made large farms impractical." You say, "Slavery is not economically viable on a small farm." In essence, work the general subject down into smaller and smaller details.

This game can be played backwards too. Start with the smallest detail you can imagine, and work your way up. Linking these various parts in your mind through the logical levels of scale helps you to remember them more easily.

Build a Flowchart

Use the symbols the way we have below and a few sheets of paper to map out your typical day. Break it down into very small steps, with as much detail as possible. When you are done, look for where your learning happens. Also look for other times or places you might learn.

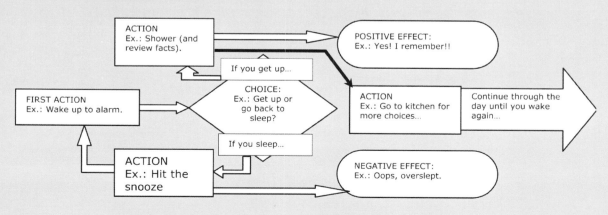

MUSICAL INTELLIGENCE - YOURS FOR A SONG

Notable Facts about Musical Intelligence

Music is felt through our ears and bodies, and it appeals to our minds. The sequentially oriented left brain experiences satisfaction because of the logical structure of the music. Simultaneously, music imparts a sense of completeness to the holistically oriented and emotional right brain.

Finally, learning researchers found that different rhythms actually change the tuning of your brain waves.

Slow music (largo, one beat per second) connects directly to our theta waves, which are associated with light sleep. In this condition, the brain is relaxed and more open to input. Slower rhythms can put us into a meditative state (alpha) while faster rhythms get our nervous system bopping into beta waves, quickening our hearts and our movements. The key to using musical intelligence for rapid learning is in uniting the physical, emotional, and logical aspects of music with what you want to learn.

Are You in Tune with Music?

Here is an assessment of how useful your musical intelligence may be. Underline the statements that apply to you. Then take note of how many of these you might also do. Doing any of these will boost your musical intelligence.

- I love music.
- I hear "music" in common sounds like traffic.
- I play music.
- I like most kinds of music.
- I remember tunes.
- I can listen to an entire song in my head.
- Rhythms move me
- I can change my mood through music.
- I have a large music collection.
- I am attracted to people with melodious voices.

Instruments to Increase Your Musical Genius

Tools	Techniques
Noisemakers	Create a sequence of sounds. Use a different noisemaker for each major step in the process or for each turning point in a history or timeline.
Natural sounds	Listen to rhythms and sounds from nature (live or recorded) as you study. Consciously link specific sounds with things you want to learn. For example, different birdcalls can be related to memorizing different state capitals.
Headphones	Using headphones to listen to lectures or lists on tape will increase focus and integration.
Favorite songs	Using familiar tunes, write lyrics containing the facts and processes you want to remember.
Any instrument	Make one tone when you begin a session, another when you are done. Create a different rhythm to symbolically signal the start and end of each new concept or chapter.
Tape or digital	Sing your lecture notes or record your own "memory rap song." Frequently, the worse your song is, the better you will remember it. Play slow music softly while you study or listen to a lecture.

Composing Something New

Find some natural rhythms that share a metaphorical relationship with your topic of study (e.g., the sound of waves relates to seashore biology). Find a way to make the information that you are learning fit this natural rhythm. Also, check these Creative References:

SuperMemory: the Revolution by Sheila Ostrander, Carroll & Graf Publishers, 1991
Sound Therapy by Peter Joudry, St Denis Publishers, 1984
http://www.optimalearning.com/optima.htm – Music-based learning
http:/www.reiinstitute.com – A great site for investigating how music affects our lives by influencing our nervous system

A Sad Song Turns Sweet

When Beth entered high school, her mother told her, "Study by sitting straight at your desk in complete silence, and take notes." Beth trusted her mother and followed the advice. Beth did poorly on the tests and rarely participated in class. One day Sally, a new friend of Beth's, invited her over to study after school. Sally's study technique was radically different; she had music blaring while they talked. They spent three hours together, reading silently to themselves, and then talking about what they had read, then talking about the music on the radio. The next day Beth was a real participant in class. She answered questions and even asked one. Her teacher was impressed and asked Beth what accounted for her learning turnaround. Beth said, "Easy. I just remember the song that was playing on the radio when I was reading a particular paragraph." The teacher looked askance but let it go because of the positive change. When Beth tried to study with the radio on at home, her mom was unhappy: "You can't study with that music blaring like that!" Beth answered, "But that's the way I've been learning so well at Sally's." After much discussion, Beth's mom got the picture and let Beth use her musical intelligence.

Rounds

All group members have a noisemaker of their choice and each person learns one part of the study topic. In round one, going around the circle, members recite each part in order. In round two, all members play their "instruments" softly as they say their parts. In round three, all members play their instruments in turn and recite the steps in their head. (This method is especially good for learning history or a process).

Your Knapsack of Noise

As a project, fill an average-size daypack with objects that make sounds you like. Visit garage sales and toy stores as well as music and department stores to find these objects. Play with rocks and springs and pieces of hardwood of different sizes. Collect some can lids and noisy wrapping paper, a thunder tube, and a nose flute.

As you collect your sound assemblage, experiment with your pack of sound-makers and record your responses. Try fast, slow, simple, and complicated rhythms and tunes. In each experiment with each sound maker, ask yourself, "What does this sound make me think or feel? You may even ask yourself, "Why do I have this response?" Most importantly, ask yourself how this response can be linked to things you want to learn. Take notes about your sounds and responses. You now have an auditory toolbox. You can use it to prepare for a learning experience in a number of ways: Make a loud noise to release your frustration before studying. Beat out the rhythm of a quadratic equation or a list of nerves or the parts of a leaf. When you want to review, make a sound to help you recall facts.

VISUAL-SPATIAL - WHERE TO GO TO SEE WHAT TO LEARN

The Science of Visual-Spatial Intelligence

Visual intelligence results from interactions between the eyes, the occipital lobe (located at the back of the brain), and the right hemisphere of the brain. Because the right brain sees wholes and contains our intuitive and emotional capabilities, visual intelligence can easily integrate ideas with feelings, making it a powerful learning tool. With the aid of the occipital lobe, visual-spatial intelligence is a powerful tool for predicting and interpreting what something might look like. Seeing someone's face from the side, I can imagine what he or she looks like from the front; seeing the city from the air, I can accurately guess what the buildings look like from the street.

Seeing Where You Are

Circle the bullet points next to the sentences that apply to you.

- I see things that other people seem to miss.
- I can use a map easily and well.
- I can recall pictures and vistas vividly.
- I doodle during lectures.
- I enjoy using different colored paper and ink.
- I experience emotional reactions to visual art.
- I remember faces well.
- I can "feel" a texture by looking at it.
- I enjoy drawing.
- Give me verbal directions, and I can see the way.

If you marked four to six of those sentences, your visual intelligence is average. Seven or eight indicates a high ability to use this intelligence. Scoring nine or above indicates that this can be a superlative tool for you to use in learning, remembering, and solving problems.

Turn on Your Visual Genius

Tools	Techniques
Colored pens & paper	Use colors to indicate each concept, question, or fact. Use a new color for a new topic.
Camera, camcorder	Take pictures of books you're studying or video a lecture.
Home or school	Study in different rooms. Consciously link important facts to colors of furniture, pictures, lamps, and windows.
Compass, templates	Adorn your notes with unique shapes. Link the key learning points with the shapes.
Art books, museums	Think about a concept you want to learn or a problem you want to solve while looking at a visual that is pleasant for you.
Colored environments	Greens and blues help you feel relaxed, red excites you, and yellow imparts a positive mood. In general, when learning, stay away from dark environments and dark colors like brown and gray because they can depress you. Also, because all-white rooms tend to make people easily distracted, they are not good environments in which to learn.

Seeing the Expansive Side

Do you try to visualize where Web sites are located geographically? Now, try to imagine some ways to visualize chunks of information, mentally bring them out of a book and picture them in another setting, such as standing around your home or classroom. More Places and Spaces

The Visual Display of Quantitative Information by Edward Tufte, Graphics Press, 2001
Visual Thinking by R. Arnheim, University of California Press, 1980
http://www.vue.org
http://www.solidprint.com/julieweb/page1.html

A Clear Story

The most difficult class for me in college was Organic Chemistry 101. Professor Sharp (I remember her name because she was such a sharp dresser) lectured rapidly while writing on the chalkboard. I took pages of notes, I studied alone and with friends, I did everything possible. Yet I got a D on the first midterm and felt terrible.

Then I made friends with a man named Amos. He did two unusual things: he took no notes, and he sat in a different seat in the room at each class. I asked him how he did on the midterm. "100 percent," he answered. "How could you?" I asked. "You don't take any notes." Amos said that he sat in a different seat every class because he looked at the ceiling tile above that seat and made a mental picture of the room as if he were suspended from the specific tile above his head. When Dr. Sharp entered the room, Amos would "take a picture" of her outfit and visualize her lecture as if she were a marionette suspended from the unique ceiling tile of that day. Then he would watch and listen with total concentration. To study for the midterm, he lay on his bed at home and visualized the unique ceiling tiles with the well-dressed professor dancing in front of the chalkboard. So prepared, Amos would then read the chalkboard of that day from memory. Amos was using his powers of concentration together with his highly active visual-spatial intelligence to record a very complicated subject perfectly. Using this technique made the exam like an open-book test for him.

Looking to Others to Help You Learn

One person reads a passage or describes a process while the others listen and draw pictures (or doodle). After ten or fifteen minutes, the reader stops and the others describe their drawings and how they relate to the learning. At the same time, the others try to duplicate the drawing without actually seeing it. In this way, each person has an opportunity to experience the visual interpretations of the others. Next, have a discussion in which you all share your drawings and explain how you translated the abstract concepts into pictures.

Going Places and Seeing Things

Sometime soon, when you are planning to take notes from a lecture or book, prepare your note pages before you take the notes. On one page draw a big red square, on another a green circle, on another a blue diamond. Try road-sign shapes, flames, and stick figures. You can even paste pictures from magazines in various parts of a note page. When you actually take notes, experiment with writing inside the shapes, outside the shapes, or across them. Try labeling a picture (of a house, for example) with the notes you take (the roof is the overall concept; the walls are ideas; the foundation, the philosophy or intent; the windows, the facts). To review (or to test yourself), draw the shapes first, and remember the information that went with them. Picture the shape with words (or more drawings) inside it before you actually look at your notes.

LINGUISTIC INTELLIGENCE - WHAT YOU SAY AND HOW YOU SAY IT

Language And The Brain

The brain-language relationship is extremely complex and powerful. It starts in the womb, where the child learns rhythms and harmony every time the mother speaks. Brain development continues through all ages. The brain creates new nodes with each new language learned. Even learning new words in your own language improves your linguistic intelligence. To pronounce a single word requires the coordination of three separate brain nodes.

- The lexical node stores meanings (Wernicke's area in the back of the language center).
- The lemma holds syntax, including case and order.
- The lexeme node stores sounds (Broca's area in the front of the language center).

These areas are all on the left side of the brain clumped around the perisylvian fissure (located behind your ear). Activity on the left side is also associated with positive emotions. The more words and languages we learn, the more linguistically smart we are. Additionally, people with larger vocabularies are perceived as being smarter than their peers.

Conversations with Yourself

If a statement is true for you, write an example of what you would enjoy doing (or what you would enjoy learning).

I read a lot. _____
I enjoy listening to a good speech. _____
I love learning new words. _____
Errors of grammar irritate me. _____
I enjoy writing. _____
Foreign accents intrigue me. _____
I like to say things well. _____
Poetry thrills me. _____
I can quote others accurately. _____

If most of these statements are true for you, then linguistic intelligence has a lot of power for you. You can learn readily through language, whether written, spoken or felt. If only a couple of the statements ring true then linguistic intelligence may not be your strong point.

Solidifying Your Linguistic Genius

Tools	Techniques
Dictionary, thesaurus	Look up definitions, synonyms, and antonyms.
Crossword puzzles	Play these word-learning games.
"Please explain more"	At every opportunity, ask speakers to add depth and complexity to their statements. They will think you are intelligent and interested. And you will learn.
Dr. Seuss books	Read them, and then parody them in a way that reinforces your learning.
Haiku, limericks	Read them, and then create new ones to help you organize the information you are studying.
Languages	Learning a new language will increase your ability to learn other things.

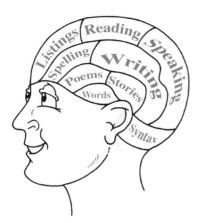

Read this Story

Aref and Mike were roommates in college. It would be difficult to find two men who were more different. Aref, a tiny Persian man who spoke horrible English, was always laughing and cracking jokes. Mike, a huge Caucasian American, was always reading and thinking serious thoughts. One day, Mike's friend David needed to replace the brake pads on his car. David approached Aref, who was a master mechanic, hoping he could get the work done and learn how to do it. By the time the first rim was unbolted, David was anxious and angry.

Aref had agreed to "show" David how to change his brake pads, which David heard as "explain." Aref was incapable of explaining anything to anyone. His verbal skills were in finding something funny in everything that happened. Fortunately, David went in the house to complain to Mike. Mike said, "Aref teaches the way he learns: by sight." And with that, Mike grabbed a manual on auto mechanics from the shelf, went with David back to the car, and began to read about brake jobs. As Aref took the wheel apart, Mike read the manual. David totally understood because he could listen to the words as he observed Aref in action. Finally, David was able to replace the brake pads on the last wheel himself. He just had to use his linguistic intelligence.

Speaking about Learning

Try playing word games focused on what you are learning. Imagine history "Scrabble"™ or chemistry "Upwords"™ or anagrams for mechanical repairs. You can also get together with your classmates to compose crossword puzzles based on the concepts you are learning, or to tell jokes, stories, or riddles using the facts you are trying to learn. For example: Q: Why did Columbus cross the ocean blue? A: To get to America in 1492. Play rhyming ping-pong in which one person tosses out a word related to what you want to learn and the other person tosses back a rhyme or turns it into a pun.

Words Are Not a Problem

As Julia Cameron says in The Artist's Way, writing in a free-flow style can have beneficial effects on your learning. Just write about it. A great practice is to write about a topic for fifteen minutes before you actually begin to study, read, hear, see, or experience it. You may find that you already know something about it. You could end up with dozens of questions – and almost as many answers – about development, users, problems, applications, and interrelationships with other things you already know.

Try a similar exercise after a learning session: close your notes; then review, relate, describe, and question what you have learned. Jot down your memories and thoughts as you go. The sequential nature of the left brain will lead you logically to what you know and don't know. After about fifteen minutes, read your new memory notes with a Hi-Liter®, checking against the text and your lecture notes for accuracy, applicability and areas where you need more facts or more conceptual information. Many people have a tough time starting to write continuously for fifteen minutes. "What will I write? How will I put it? I don't have anything to say." Never mind; just do it!

BODY INTELLIGENCE - FEEL IT WORKING

The Science of the Body-Kinesthetic intelligence

The bizarre thing related to this intelligence is that proprioception (the sense of body position, feeling, and movement) is denigrated in schools. A whopping 75 percent of high school dropouts are kinesthetic learners who are unable to find a use for their intelligence in school outside of sports.

Also, we use a lot of drugs such as aspirin, antacids, and alcohol, all of which reduce our sense of feeling.

Every part of the body has nerve endings. All of these nerve endings are continually sending messages up the spinal column, and they are combined in the medulla located at the top of the spinal column just inside the skull. Filtering these sensations is the big job of the reticular formation in the brain stem. There is so much information that if you paid attention to all the sensations that fill your body, you would not be able to do anything else. Kinesthetic learning links learning to movement and sensation by hitching a ride on this flow of information.

Moving with Yourself

For each statement, try two things. First, write when and where you last did the activity, and second, mime the activity (even if someone is watching).

ACTIVITY   **WHERE & WHEN**

Effective throwing: _____
Flexible movements: _____
Good balancing: _____
Small and precise movements: _____
Enjoyment of being in my body: _____
Building things: _____
Exercising: _____
Engaging in fun chores: _____
Trusting a gut feeling: _____
Learning by doing: _____

- If you have done two or three of these recently and felt comfortable in your movements, you are average in your use of this intelligence.
- Between four and six puts you at the top thirty percent of the population.
- If you are comfortable with more than six of the ten statements, then body-kinesthetic intelligence will be very useful to you in learning.

Exercise Your Body Genius

Tools	Techniques
Clay, blocks, cards	Build something while learning. Think how the clay, blocks, or cards might relate to the learning material (e.g., use clay to make a cannon while learning about Napoleon).
Flow chart on floor	Draw the process you want to learn on 3x5 cards or bigger sheets; then walk on the process to learn it.
Dance, yoga	Create a new dance movement. Then associate steps or postures with the new concepts (e.g., use hands and feet, your own and others, to represent atoms or the flow of history).
Ball, rosary	Play with something while learning. Just moving it around in your hand will help you remember.

Explorations

Go for a walk and bring your learning along with you. If you are learning about history, think (as you walk) about how that history affected your world. If you are studying chemistry, look for the use and the results of those chemical processes in the world around you. Also, wander over to

Influencing with Integrity by Genie Z. Laborde, Syntony, 1984
Multiple Intelligences by Spencer Kagan and Michael Kagan, Kagan Cooperative Learning, CA 1998
http://www.dance.ohio-state.edu/~dnb/LabanLab/
http://www.braingym.com

A Feel-Good Story

Brenda was a terrible student. Labeled ADHD and hyperactive, she simply could not sit still in a classroom. She was given drugs for hyperactivity, but those just made her listless. Brenda's parents tried everything, but nothing helped.

Brenda was invited to go surfing and was soon hooked. She loved balancing on the board and the pull of her arms as she paddled out. She even loved the wipeouts. Her new friend was in college and often studied on the beach while waiting for the waves to change. When Brenda began studying there also, her friend suggested that she take notes. "OK," Brenda said, "but I don't have any paper." The friend gave her a permanent marker and suggested that she write on her surfboard.

Brenda read two pages of algebra and wrote five formulas on her surfboard. When the waves improved, she headed for the water. When she caught a wave, she would walk around on the formulas. When she fell, she would see the formulae flying over her head. The next week at school was a shock for everyone: Brenda got a B on the test. From then on, Brenda wrote notes everywhere. If it moved and she could move with it, she would write on it. She had history dates on her steering wheel and English notes on the door of her room. Her parents were distressed at first, but when they saw her grades, they let Brenda write on whatever she wanted.

Circles & Squares

Go with some friends to a folk dance, square dance, Sufi dance, or line-dance. Learn a dance sequence together.

When you get back home, practice this dance sequence while reciting ideas, facts, or processes that you are learning. You will quickly associate the turns, touches, stomps, and skips with your learning objectives. To review your learning, move around in your study area – or you can just imagine dancing around the room as you review your topic.

Work It Out

Try at least three of the following suggestions to bring more movement and feeling into your learning.

- Build a model or plant a garden. Relate the parts to your learning.
- Make up your own sign language to represent concepts or facts.
- Exercise for three minutes between reading sections.
- Study while using a Nautilus machine or riding a stationary bike.
- Use a different sitting or standing or lying posture for each section read.
- Associate the material you're learning with common actions (e.g., driving a car, drying off after a shower, turning on your radio, washing dishes).
- Climb around on a jungle gym or tree while reviewing your assignment.

NATURALISTIC - INTELLIGENCE, NATURALLY

Natural Science

When Lucy roamed the plains of Africa four million years ago, naturalistic intelligence was life. Our ancient ancestors depended on it to know the habits of game and to learn the whereabouts of water and a secure habitat. Now, for most of us in the English-speaking world, being in nature is an oddity (as in a camping vacation). Instead of being a practice of life, ecology is a special field of study chosen by only a few people.

Despite this, naturalistic intelligence is one of the two comprehensive intelligences. It is connected to all that we are. Since we are natural creatures, everything we do is natural. As natural creatures, we exhibit patterns shown in all living things. We eat, rest, move, and respond to stimulus. Fundamental brain mechanisms, such as fear and nurturing, are identical across species. We now understand that effective learners actively observe, reflect upon, and move with the ever-changing world of nature.

What Is the Nature of Your Intelligence?

Which of these apply to you?

- I have pets.
- I enjoy gardening.
- I know the names of many local trees.
- I sometimes compare myself to a particular animal.
- I frequently use words such as stream, growth, and branch-out when talking about activities (e.g., "We need to grow the business").
- I care about the ecology of my area.
- I like to go camping or hunting.
- I use nature metaphors (e.g., "Let's nurture this idea") when I talk.

If four of the above statements apply to you, then you have an average naturalistic intelligence. If you said yes to five or more statements, your use of naturalistic intelligence will be a powerful tool to grow your memory.

Becoming a Genius in and of Nature

Tools	Techniques
Houseplants	Notice how stems branch and seek the light. Relate this to how you might outline your study information.
Yard plants	Notice how every species has its own season. Relate this to the timing of historical events or reactions.
Pets	Figure out how their behaviors are similar to what you are studying.
Trees	Map your knowledge: the trunk is the topic, branches are ideas, leaves are facts. Track the branching of evolution or ideas.
Nature movies	Observe the adaptability of animals. How will you adapt to changes in your environment or your new genius?

Exploring Nature

Whatever animals learn becomes ingrained in their lives. Consider all the animals you've seen or heard about. Which one is most like you? Observe that animal, live or on tape. Watch how it eats, plays, and lives. If you were that animal, what would you do to make your learning ingrained? You can also explore:

Thoreau: People, Principles and Politics by Henry David Thoreau, Milton Meltzer, ed., Hill and Wang, 1963
http://www.primenet.com/~brendel

One Natural Step

Mazie is president of an organization dedicated to preserving wetlands. The group started by preserving six acres and now wants to preserve 9,994 more. Mazie spoke to several groups, but when she talked about the size of their vision, people's eyes glazed over and their checkbooks remained closed.

In thinking about the fauna of the region, Mazie remembered the marsh wren. This bird nests in the tall reeds of the wetlands. The newly hatched chicks have an extremely limited world; they see only stems and a bit of sky until they grow and develop their flying feathers. At six weeks, the fledglings are ready to clear the reeds with their own wings.

"Imagine what the young bird sees as it clears the undergrowth for the first time," Mazie extolled at a meeting of potential supporters. "A huge expanse of world filled with trees and rivers and a sky as big as it was blue! This is where our foundation is now." The audience was spellbound. People could relate to the stems and underbrush; then, they could see the sky "as big as it was blue," and, using their naturalistic intelligence, they learned what the foundation was trying to do. They gave with all the generosity of a mother wren.

Be Natural With Your Friends

It's easy and fun to accentuate your naturalistic intelligence in study groups. First, remember that you are all natural creatures with movement, rhythms, abilities, and needs. Start by studying outdoors wherever you can – or by watching nature videos. Watch the shadows change as time passes. Notice that a shadow was here while you were discussing one formula and then over there when you applied it to an architectural problem. After you have been studying together for a while, take a break and observe something natural like trees, a garden, or the sky. Relate what you are seeing, smelling, and hearing now to what you are learning. For example, leaves clump together much the way molecules do. See a group of facts as a flock of birds; see eggs and sperm as chemical elements coming together. Challenge one another to see how well you each can make a natural metaphor fit your learning process.

Do This Until It Feels Natural

Nature is about living and dying and changing. Everything has its own natural lifespan. Thinking about a lifespan is simply to imagine (1) how something came into being; (2) the rhythms observed through time and seasons; (3) the degradation of the thing; and (4) the transition of the thing into something else. When you want to study a computer program draw a cartoon representation of the lifespan of the program: what happens when it is booted up, how does it live, and when does it get turned off and die.

This lifespan can be similar to any natural thing you enjoy, such as a tree or an animal. Associate the steps or ideas of the computer program with the four phases mentioned above, labeling your cartoon sequence with the logical steps of the subject. Review it by recreating the cartoon and re-labeling its panels with the information to be remembered. This exercise is simple and often humorous.

EXISTENTIAL INTELLIGENCE - TO RECONNECT

The Science of the Spiritual

Each nerve cell in the frontal lobes of your brain (directly behind your forehead) has thousands of axons and dendrites (senders and receivers), so each cell is connected with thousands of other cells in the frontal lobes. This nerve cell, with its multiplexed linkages, almost creates a world of its own, a world that is perfect for imagining options, creating jokes, and maintaining a sense of our spiritual connection to everything. The frontal lobes of the human brain may be the most complicated things in the universe.

It is sometimes difficult to learn a new skill because we feel that we must understand it before we actually do it. That understanding is done with our frontal lobes. Yet, unlike most of the brain, the frontal lobes are not concerned about controlling the body. So an important part of the learning process is to consciously use the frontal lobes to teach the mid brain how to control the muscles and tendons that will actually do the activity.

The frontal lobes also contribute to learning by attributing meaning and significance. Every culture on Earth has invented deities, spirits, and the stories that accompany them. All of this helps humans to make sense of the confusing world in which we live. This, "quest for connection" is not only part of how we learn, it is also part of why we learn.

Karma Connection

Basically, existential thinkers believe that

- There are reasons for things, even when they make no sense to us.
- Everything that is and everything that happens has meaning and purpose, even if we are unable to figure it out.
- Some things, such as wands, books, symbols, and clothes, are sacred and must be treated with extra respect, even reverence.
- What we are doing is right, and it should not even be questioned.
- Gratitude to the natural or supernatural is always appropriate.
- If we are good, we can ask for supernatural help.

To find your level of attunement, look for those six beliefs in your thinking about everyday things. Do you have special or sacred do-dads on your desk or computer? Do you see deeper meaning in the way a garden grows or the sink stops up? Do you ask for help when there's no one around? Do you tell yourself that no matter what's gone wrong, things will work out for the best eventually (thy will be done)? When you find yourself using these tricks of the frontal lobes, rejoice! You can use all aspects of this type of thinking to learn language, logic, logarithms, literature, leadership, or Lord knows what.

"There Are No Atheists during Final Exams." –Anonymous

Tools	Techniques
Rituals, incantations	Repeat what you're learning with a holy tone or rhythm. Pray for fast assimilation before and after a learning session. Cast a spell on the material – ask (or tell) it to go into your memory.
Yoga or other moves	Integrate new learning with your body by making religious gestures or movements that have deeper meaning.
Churches, mosques, etc.	Go to holy places to learn; define the library as a place of worship.
Learning rituals	Create rituals. Be thankful, atone, ask for help.

What Lies beyond Religion?

There is a branch of Hinduism that believes the path to Brahman and eternal bliss is laughter. The devotees of this sect laugh together as their morning prayer. This makes sense, because laughter is a function of the frontal lobes. Morihei Ueshiba, the inventor of aikido, said, "I am the universe," as are we all. One major function of religion is to explain creation – you also have the ability to create. How are you a universe unto yourself? How are your classmates a universe? What new ways of learning can you create within your universe?

http://www.Koran.org
http://www.chaordic.org
http://www.gmu.edu/org/hsc/hindu_res.html

Building Meaning

Donna was trying to learn the names of the rocks in part of Arizona. She was often confused about the composition and hardness of the various stones. A friend of Donna's gathered similar rocks into piles and labeled them with a felt pen. She suggested that Donna might make a pile with softer rocks on top and harder ones on the bottom.

When Donna piled her rocks against a large boulder to study them, she recognized that she had an altar. It was almost as if she had formed a new religion, just for the study of geology. The big boulder was the god of rocks. The others were angel rocks with different powers of hardness. She then created a ritual of throwing the rocks against the boulder, saying their name as she did so. Each rock made a slightly different sound that Donna would note. She'd say "Hallelujah" or "Amen" or "Praise the Lord (of Rocks)" every time she threw a rock and recognized its sound.

Gettin' That Old-Time Religion

While meaning and significance are conjured in the frontal lobes, religions are social. You can capitalize on this phenomenon by creating a "religion" from your studies.

Say we want to make a religion to help us learn Windows 98 ™. First, we decide who will be our deity (Bill Gates?). Then we talk about all the marvelous things this deity has done for us (because he loves us!). Now, get together and make rituals out of the learning and perform them solemnly. You can imagine the computer lab is a temple and the books have precious traditions given to us by the magically endowed priests who are in contact with our deity. Anything we don't fully understand and must still learn we chalk up to supernatural powers or "this god works in strange ways;" then we must learn more scripture!

A Religious Experience

Consider learning to be a magical activity loaded with meaning, significance, and power. As you study this book, try pretending that it is magical, loaded with mystical spells. Just as the eardrum seems to magically change sound into electrical impulses that your brain can understand, this book can magically help you learn. To enhance its power, try keeping this book someplace special. In addition to your other reading, remember to read this book on special days. Make your desk into an altar and your learning tools into sacred objects. You may even dress in a long colorful robe to study. Next, create prayers, meditations, songs, or chants to repeat before, during, and after your study time. Now, speak aloud your own words of goodness, power, importance, and need. Conjure up a friendly leprechaun that will help you learn. Ask it to lead you through the pages of your books to find the hidden pot of gold, nirvana, or redemption. Similarly, place a call to your guardian angel. Ask him or her to protect you from distractions and all things that make learning difficult or painful. Remember to give thanks for all the benefits you receive.

CREATIVE INTELLIGENCE - ALLOW THE TIME

Creative Facts

There are really three types of creative intelligence (CI).

- Extrapolative CI uses techniques such as brainstorming, exploration, and mind mapping to create new ideas by building on existing ones. Increasing your level of stimulation or information enhances this intelligence.
- Interpolative CI uses techniques of relaxation, meditation, journal writing, random drawing, and collage-type art projects to find linkages between things that you already know. You can bring out this intelligence with quiet and contemplation.
- Conversion is the form of CI that uses metaphor, poetry, comedy, and acting to change the relationship between things. Poetry, for example, can reduce the journey of a lifetime into a small choice about which road to take when walking through the woods.

Although your preference may lean toward one specific CI, you will find that you switch back and forth between all three as you go through the creative process.

Dare I be Creative?

How creative are you? Creativity is the rarest and most difficult to measure of the intelligences. We all have significant amounts of creativity floating around in our heads. If you have fluffy bunches of the stuff, you might often find yourself

- lost in a book
- daydreaming
- easily influenced by movies
- doodling while you talk on the phone
- making pictures on your math notes
- making up really good excuses
- thinking of new ideas as you fall asleep
- coming up with new ideas, jokes, and puns
- being reminded of other things

If you do any of these – or any one of a thousand other things that don't seem to make much sense – than you have the special gift of creativity.

Creativity Made Easy

Tools	Techniques
Magazines	Make a collage that summarizes your learning.
Paper	Write poems about your learning.
Quiet	Relax for ten minutes before and after studying a subject. Just watch your learning float by like clouds.
Friends	Make a one-act play that describes what you are learning. Actors might be historical figures, steps in a process, molecules, or anything.
Point of view	Look at your learning from different perspectives. Reverse, combine, change size, adjust time, or change the shape of the information. Ask "what if" questions and think up answers that are real or wacky.

Creativity Squared

How do you get creative about creativity? Well, you start by exploring outward as far as you can – and then going a little further. Try a random Web search; then find ways to link the results to your learning – the weirder the better. Here are some sites and a book to get you going.

A Whack in the Side of the Head by Roger von Oech, Warner Books, 1998
http://www.randomwebsearch.com/index.html
http://www.globalideasbank.org/index.html

Steve's Story

When Chance Massaro came to me with his idea for a book on learning, I had to take it one step further. Rather than a book that contained hundreds of pages of boring text, I suggested one that used graphics and layout to help people learn. Chance agreed enthusiastically, and we began.

Typically, Chance did the writing while I edited or rewrote material as needed. I learned an amazing amount of information by using one of my favorite intelligences – creativity. I learned by rewriting, essentially recreating all the information in a way that seemed to make sense to me.

In order to recreate the information successfully, I had to wrap my mind around it, discuss it with Chance, draw pictures, write it in my own words, and rewrite it until it looked right. I also had to relate this new information to things I already knew.

Mass Creativity

Creativity can be like a spark flying between individuals. Every time it strikes, it can spark more creative thought for the whole group. Since one form of creativity involves linking information, you can play Information Tag.

In this game, one person tosses out a fact from your studies and the next person must come up with a fact that is linked to it. Use dates, quotes, chemical bonds, or whatever might be linked. Map the information on a big sheet of paper; you'll be amazed at the results.

Creating Your Own Future

Creativity is also used when imagining a vision for your future. Let's take some time to exercise your creativity by looking into your future.

1. First, get four pieces of paper.
2. On one page, write a short paragraph describing the past ten years of your life – what you did and what you loved.
3. On another sheet, write a short paragraph about where you are now. Include the things you like to do, people that bring out strong feelings for you, and your hopes and fears for the future.
4. On the third sheet, write a longer paragraph about where you want to be ten years from now. Where you will live, what will your house be like, what type of people will you be with?
5. Using the last piece of paper, draw 10 stair steps. On the bottom step write "today". On the top step write "10 years from now". On each step, write what you will need to do to get to the next step above it.
6. Finally, think for a few minutes about the things you want to learn to get to the top of the stairs. If it seems overwhelming, just remember that today you only need to learn a small part of that, just a tiny step.
7. As you learn, remind yourself from time to time of your goal at each step and how your learning will get you there.

YOUR_____ INTELLIGENCE

This Section Is Different.

We have covered as many modalities and intelligences as possible in the limits of this book, but we couldn't cover all of them. This section gives you an opportunity to create your own personal intelligence style. Choose a name for your intelligence and write it at the top of the page. Choose something you are good at, something you enjoy. It might be

- car-repair intelligence
- cooking intelligence
- model railroading intelligence
- reading intelligence
- time intelligence
- baseball intelligence

Think of what works for you.

Then, follow the instructions at the top of each box and fill in the blanks so that this section resembles others you have read (if you have difficulty, go back and check others for examples). Write it so that others can read it and get it quickly and easily. By doing this exercise, you'll learn more about yourself and how you can learn to learn.

The Science

Write a brief history of this special intelligence. What were its origins? How many different tasks or aspects can be associated with it?

_____
_____
_____
_____
_____
_____
_____
_____
_____

Self-Assessment

List three to five positive personal traits that help make you really good at what you do.

_____
_____
_____
_____
_____
_____
_____
_____
_____
_____
_____
_____
_____
_____
_____

Your Questions

How long have you been using this intelligence?

_____

What other intelligences does this one support?

_____

Does it get in the way of other intelligences?

_____

What would you suggest to others who wanted to gain or use this intelligence?

_____
_____

Exercises and Tools for Easily Increasing Your Memory and Genius

List five or more things you associate with this special intelligence and how you can use those things in various activities to help you learn more easily (turn back to previous activities sections for some ideas).

_____
_____
_____
_____
_____
_____

Draw a picture here that represents your special intelligence. You might show objects that are used with this intelligence, yourself engaged in the activity, something that is representative of the intelligence, or even an abstract drawing.

Your Creativity

Where do you see yourself going in the next ten years with this skill or hobby?

_____
_____
_____

What will you need to learn to get there? _____
_____
_____

How might you use your special intelligence to learn what you need to know? _____
_____
_____
_____
_____
_____
_____
_____

Your Story

Write a short story about a time when you used your special intelligence to learn something new.

_____
_____
_____
_____
_____
_____
_____
_____
_____
_____
_____
_____
_____

With Your Best Friends

Who else do you know that has this type of special intelligence? _____
_____

When you get together, what is there about the way you talk and relate that allows you to use this intelligence effectively? _____
_____

How might you more purposefully use that aspect of your relationship to learn more together now? _____
_____

What might others do to use this intelligence to learn something new?_____
_____

Your Exercise

Write a step-by-step process that you can use to

1) bring information in more easily
_____

2) consciously link it to something you already know or do _____
_____

3) draw the information out again when you want it _____
_____

TEN FAVORITE INTELLIGENCES

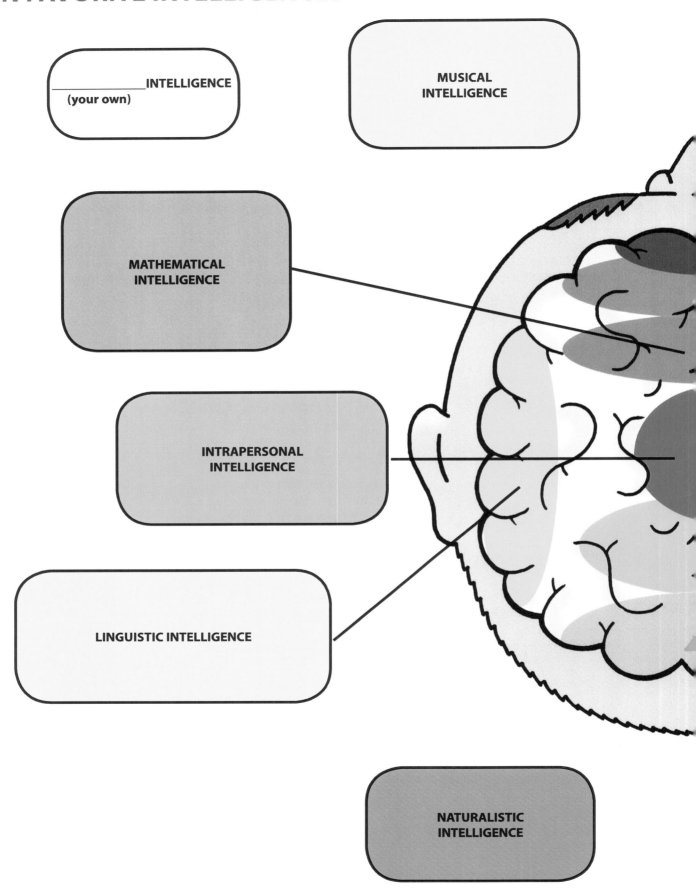

_____INTELLIGENCE
(your own)

MUSICAL
INTELLIGENCE

MATHEMATICAL
INTELLIGENCE

INTRAPERSONAL
INTELLIGENCE

LINGUISTIC INTELLIGENCE

NATURALISTIC
INTELLIGENCE

Write in your favorite techniques on these pages. See where your strengths and weaknesses are. Combine techniques that use your strengths to improve the weaker areas.

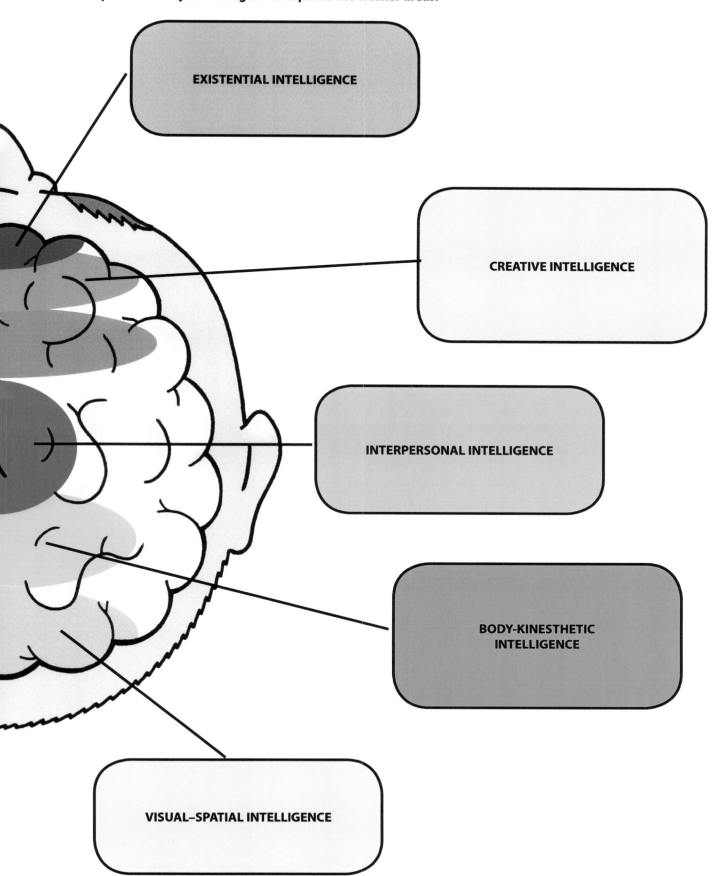

EXISTENTIAL INTELLIGENCE

CREATIVE INTELLIGENCE

INTERPERSONAL INTELLIGENCE

BODY-KINESTHETIC INTELLIGENCE

VISUAL–SPATIAL INTELLIGENCE

CHAPTER FOUR

BRAIN CLICK

Our senses bring information in, our intelligences integrate the information and make sense of it. Our "cognitive patterns" influence what we easily DO with new information. While each of us can become proficient at every pattern, most of us tend to lean on one or two. Steve is a synthetic thinker and a hardworking pragmatist. Chance tends toward synthetic and realist thinking.

SYNTHESIST

"Let's look at how things fit together in the big picture."

In this chapter, we clicked on ideas and insights from Carol Goman, Burton Cisco, Samuel Messick, Allen Harrison, and Robert Bramson.

ANALYST

"I want to take it apart and see how it works."

IDEALIST

"Here's what I think will happen next…"

REALIST

"I'm just looking at the facts."

PRAGMATIST

"Let's do it!"

There are five basic styles that your brain uses to think. To find your preferred cognitive style(s), read the following statements. Use ten points for each question and divide those points among the possible answers in a way that works best for you. For example, in statement #1, if "abrupt and to the point" is totally you, and none of the other answers seem to relate to you at all, you might give that answer ten points and give nothing to the others. Or, if all the answers seem to apply equally to you, you might divide the points more equally, giving two to each of the five answers.

1. I am most likely to impress others as
_____ (a) abrupt and to the point
_____ (b) judgmental about future events
_____ (c) logical and analytical
_____ (d) intellectual and complex
_____ (e) open-minded and adaptable

2. When I am learning something new, I am successful with
_____ (a) the hands-on approach
_____ (b) speculating about where the ideas could go
_____ (c) following a systematic plan
_____ (d) speculation about where ideas came from
_____ (e) playing with different approaches as I go along

3. When I think about solving a problem, I
_____ (a) concentrate on what I can see, hear, or touch
_____ (b) focus on the people involved
_____ (c) analyze what caused the problem
_____ (d) study the underlying ideas and relationships
_____ (e) act as soon as I can

IDEALIST

"Here's what I think will happen next…"

SYNTHESIST

"Let's look at how things fit together in the big picture."

4. When I'm frustrated with new points of view, I relax by
_____ (a) bringing in an expert to help me
_____ (b) imagining where this knowledge might lead
_____ (c) logically understanding all the parts
_____ (d) integrating the new view with existing knowledge
_____ (e) finding ways to use the new perspective

5. When learning something new, I value
_____ (a) information based on people's experience
_____ (b) the most recent discoveries
_____ (c) new knowledge based on facts, statistics, and data
_____ (d) a variety of information sources
_____ (e) learning things that I can employ now

PRAGMATIST

"Let's do it!"

ANALYST

"I want to take it apart and see how it works."

6. When teaching something to someone, I tend to leave out
_____ (a) the abstract
_____ (b) the math or the detailed proof
_____ (c) anything emotional
_____ (d) the trivial details
_____ (e) what came before or what comes after

Add up the points you marked for each "a" answer and write that total below. Do the same for the other letters. This will show you your cognitive style.

_____ (a) Realist: mostly concerned with what is
_____ (b) Idealist: mostly concerned with what will be
_____ (c) Analyst: logically taking things apart
_____ (d) Synthesist: finding relationships
_____ (e) Pragmatist: interested in how things can be used

REALIST

"I'm just looking at the facts."

Think about your strengths in learning and your opportunities to improve as you go through this chapter.

Assessment adapted from *Managing for Commitment* by Carol Goman, Ph.D.

REALIST - STRAIGHT AND NARROW

The Science

Scientifically speaking, realists use their left-brain with strong linkages to the limbic system. Give them enough facts and examples and realists will learn quickly and surely.

But once the realist has learned something, it can be difficult for him or her to entertain divergent points of view or conflicting information. This is because the natural filter in the realist's brain is closed to all but what is considered to be real.

The "Real" Thinker

Fill in the blanks below quickly.

To learn a computer program I need_____ to make sure that what I am learning is real.

To learn geometry I want to see _____ to fully accept the theory.

To learn how government works I need to talk with_____ to get the straight scoop.

If these questions were easy for you to answer, you know what kind of reality you need to help you learn. This shows a disposition toward realist thinking.

Increase your Realist Memory with these Tools and Techniques

Tools	Techniques
Newspaper, current magazines	Use eyewitness accounts to learn how the topic you are studying may be applied.
Documentaries	See exactly what was experienced; imagine what those experiences must have felt like to those involved. Then, use those feelings to anchor the facts you are trying to learn.
Recorded lectures	Hear it as it actually was.

REALIST

"I'm just looking at the facts."

Lynn's Story

Lynn makes many of us uncomfortable with her endless stories. When you ask Lynn, "How are things?" she will tell you the health and activities of her husband and all her kids. Ask her about her day and she begins with, "I got out of bed and went straight to the kitchen and . . ."

If you say, "Yesterday we went to the beach and had a great time," Lynn wants to know when you left, how long it took you to get there, and every action you took while there. We all agree that Lynn could never tell a lie; she's too committed to the factual experiences of real life. Although some of us might become bored with such a profusion of details, Lynn is clearly concerned with the facts. She is also very much a realist.

Real People

Enjoy a common experience with your group. This might be an activity, meal, learning experience, or movie. Then, sit in a circle and have each person recount the entire experience in relation to what he or she saw, heard, or actually did.

Don't allow generalities, assumptions, suppositions, or even judgments. Encourage each person to use only concrete examples. Instead of "She ran really fast" insist on "yards per second" or some other absolute measurement. Listen until everyone is bored, because the longer you listen (especially if the material is difficult), the more you build your realist cognitive style.

If your group is learning something new, call in an expert who can tell you all exactly where the information came from, who did the research, and so forth.

You can also check the sources to find out the unvarnished truth; look for the footnotes, endnotes, and references.

Don't stop there. Conduct experiments as a group to find out for yourselves.

A Super Simple Realistic Thinking Exercise

For an entire day – or as long as you can – notice and be suspicious of the verb "to be."

When you listen to people talk, stop them whenever they use "is," "am," or "are," and ask for examples and details. Ask in a gentle way: "How do you know?" You'll get lots of extra facts – and become an expert in thinking like a realist. The more facts you have, the easier it is to link them together and learn.

PRAGMATIC - LET'S GET MOVING

Science in Action

The left frontal lobe is very active in pragmatists. This lobe has many linkages with the motor sensors and the mid-brain. Pragmatic thinking is practical, right-now thinking, leading to beneficial action.

Pragmatics are rarely deep, thorough, or futuristic in their thinking. When pragmatists want to learn something, they want to see how what they're learning can be used today. They may be thoroughly uninterested in the theories behind the directions or their implications, unless they are clearly linked to actions.

Action–Thinking

For immediate learning about your pragmatism, complete these sentences.

It will be easy for me to learn this software program if _____.

I will learn these formulae best by _____.

Procedures are easy for me to remember because _____.

Don't share theories with me unless _____.

Look at your responses and compare them with the information about pragmatic thinkers in the other boxes. How pragmatic a thinker are you?

If you are very pragmatic, go apply that insight immediately. Close this book and go do something that will reinforce your learning.

If you are not very pragmatic, you can build your pragmatic cognition by reading more of this page and trying some of the techniques.

Obvious Steps to Building a Pragmatic Memory

Tools	Techniques
Everything you must learn	Find a way to use it as soon as possible.
Step-by-step directions, checklists	Just do it now, by the book.
Modeling a successful doer	Don't ask why; just do what they did.
Role-playing or acting a script	Just follow the prescribed path word for word.
The teacher's role	If the subject is too abstract to use immediately, you must become a teacher and help someone else learn the information.
Books	Try reading one paragraph at a time. As soon as you find something that you can do, go do it.

PRAGMATIST

"Let's do it!"

Be Creative with Your Pragmatism

If you are a strong pragmatic thinker, does creativity really apply to you? Yes it does. But it helps if it is creativity in motion.

Take what you are learning and make your own set of how-to instructions; then follow them – immediately. You can also think back to a time when you could have used the information. Take a minute to imagine how you might have used the information to make your life better. Try asking other people how they do common things like brushing their teeth or peeling an orange. What can you learn?

The Story of Lars

Lars loved to tell me stories about how often and how quickly he would repair the assembly line. Talking to others at the plant, I heard a different story.

Managers had a hard time with Lars. It seemed that in his team, he was the most frequently requested engineer when someone needed to solve a problem on the manufacturing floor. Other engineers would say, "Let me study this and I'll get back to you." But this was frustrating for the assemblers, who wanted to get the line moving. Lars would get the assembly line back up and running in record time. Of course, Lars's quick fixes rarely lasted long, so assemblers would have to call him back again soon. Also, they never got to the root of the problem.

Lars's supervisor teamed him up with an analytic thinker for a month, and the work of both improved as they looked at the same problem from two styles of thinking. Although for the first two weeks, each thought the other was from another planet.

Working Together

Get a bunch of friends together and talk about the games they like to play – sports, board games, cards, or whatever.

Discuss each game as if it were a practical means to an end as opposed to something fun to do. For example, football teaches strategy and endurance, chess teaches spatial intelligence, darts build hand-eye coordination, and so on. It can be funny, and you can also use this technique to help bring relevance to your other learning.

Take any subject and talk about how applicable it will be in real life. This may be scary for some teachers, when the learning is abstract knowledge. Your challenge is to figure out ways that you will use even the abstract knowledge in meaningful ways.

How Can I Use This?

When people in our culture converse, there is a conspiracy to avoid silence. For some reason, the quiet seems uncomfortable to most people. As soon as one person stops talking, the other person starts. The first step in this game is to stop. When someone asks, "How are you?" avoid the usual response. Instead, stop for a moment and ask yourself how various responses might serve you in the moment. For example, if you tell about a strange pain you have, you might bring out some sympathy or a suggestion for therapy. If you describe your excitement about an upcoming project, you might make the other person excited or jealous. If you don't answer at all, the other person might get angry or repeat the question.

All of these responses and many, many more are potential experiences. Consider how many experiences you miss simply because you don't see an immediate use for them. By taking the time to stop and experience, we grow. By taking the time to create more and different experiences, we grow even more.

SYNTHETIC - PUT IT TOGETHER

The Science of Synthesis

Scientifically speaking, synthetic thinkers are whole brain thinkers. Women tend to be far more synthetic than men in their thinking. First, because the bundle of nerves that links the left and right brains (corpus collosum) is twice as big in women as in men. Women find it easy to think logically about food combinations while nurturing a baby, for example. Second, women are acculturated to take care of others, which means that they are likely to feel comfortable with different cultures and styles.

Synthetic thinking can seem scattered. Sometimes it's hard to get the synthesist to stay on one topic because he or she can be constantly realizing other ideas that relate to the subject at hand. Of all the cognition styles, people with this one are the most easily distracted; whole brain thinking can go anywhere.

Interactive

Recognize and build your synthetic cognitive style by playing this game.

Just draw random lines from the words on the right to fill in a blank on the left.

I'm learning _____at home.	Snow White
I'm learning _____ at work.	bulldozer
I'm learning _____ spiritually.	song birds
I'm learning _____ materially.	space travel
I'm learning _____ physically.	Da Vinci
I'm learning _____ for my career.	fingerprints
I'm learning _____ emotionally.	warm sweater
I'm learning _____ recreationally.	elevator buttons
I'm learning _____ socially.	iceberg
I'm learning _____ financially.	molecules

Then think about how the two might somehow relate. Goofy? Funny? Mnemonic? Surely synthetic. For example, if I end up with "I'm learning elevator buttons for my career," I might link different stories of the building to different chapters of a book. I could even visit a tall building and get out on the different floors to look around and find something to anchor my learning with my experience. If this exercise is fun for you, then your brain has those elements that combine to create a strong synthetic cognitive style.

A Collection of Methods for Improving Your Synthetic Memory

Tools	Techniques
Stories, poems, and plays	Translate what you're learning (e. g., chemistry, computer programs) into a story, or act it out.
Dartboard	Place your notes on a dartboard and throw three darts at them. Each dart will hit a different piece of information. Your job is to think of how to link that information. The process of linking will help you learn.
The world and beyond	In person, or in your mind by using maps, go and see or imagine how your subject is being used, anywhere and everywhere.

SYNTHESIST

"Let's look at how things fit together in the big picture."

Be Creative with your Synthetic Learning

Our philosophy is that everything is connected to everything. So there are dozens of ways that you can be creative with synthetic learning. Just stay conscious and joyous through this process.

Visit websites you're not interested in, and think of the relationships they could have to what you are learning. Go into a library, pick out five books from five different sections, and open them to random pages while you study your subject. Take your learning to the street corner, the swale, the forest, or the beach. Talk with a child about what you are learning; ask a businessman what he thinks about your study. For some of us this will be painful because it seems irrelevant.

Steve's Story

Steve is the coauthor of this book. He is an idea generator of the first magnitude. The reason is simple: Steve thinks synthetically. Everything reminds him of something else. He is always making leaps of logic that the rest of us can't imagine.

Steve is a classic synthetic guided by human enhancement values. Every day Steve comes up with a new idea about how to get people together to make life more fun, more spiritually fulfilling, and more economically worthwhile. I note gently that many people are disoriented by Steve's imagination, his willingness to connect "outside the box."

When asked how he remembers all these things, Steve replies, "I don't. If there are enough linkages, the information just pops up because it's related to the topic under discussion." One unusual thing about Steve is that he is committed to follow-through. When he comes up with a great idea, and some folks see its value and are willing to pursue it, Steve will do the legwork to make it happen.

Friendly Hyperbole

Dancing trees? The brains of a screwdriver? A bruise as big as Rhode Island? The sky is falling?

The game is called "hyperbole" and can be played with any number of people who are learning the same thing. The idea is to take what you are learning and make it into an outrageous exaggeration. Take a concept, such as names of body parts, and make each one totally goofy and huge. You'll remember the parts by the loony comparisons.

For example, the hippocampus is a horseshoe-shaped piece of gray matter sitting at the bottom of your brain. It processes auditory information and has its own short-term memory. I remember this by thinking of a hippo wearing horseshoes, camping out at the bottom of my brain. He likes to hear stories but doesn't remember them for long.

An Exercise in Synthetic Thinking

Plastic is the most common synthetic in our culture. It all comes from oil. It can be fashioned into long-lasting fence-posts or flimsy grocery bags. Look at all the plastic things you come into to contact with throughout your day and relate them to a single discipline (for example, chemistry or economics) you are currently learning. See if you can relate qualities of the plastics with qualities of the discipline.

Let's say you're learning geography. First, make a list of all the plastic things around you. Then, relate each geographic fact with a different plastic item. To help remember the fact, think about what and where the related plastic thing is.

IDEALIST - THE POWER TO PREDICT

What the Science Will Be

Scientifically speaking, idealists are left-brain, sequential thinkers who logically deduce the future by noting current trends. Though the name suggests a Pollyanna-like, rose-colored-glasses viewpoint, these folks are more logical than optimistic. When they look at the current situation, they try to figure out what the future will be, positive or negative. Idealists generally demonstrate a high degree of interpersonal intelligence and can relate to the feelings and desires of others. While these folks set high standards, they are generally not good with details. They also tend to avoid conflict; their mind is made up, so they see no reason to argue.

Your Worst and Best Futures

Look at each of the life arenas below and think about what has happened to you in the past twelve months and where you are now. Then, on the left side, write the worst thing you can reasonably expect to happen to you in that arena within the coming year. Next, on the right side, write the best result you can reasonably expect in the next twelve months.

Worst Future	Arena	Best Future
_____	Finances	_____
_____	Recreation	_____
_____	Family	_____
_____	Career	_____
_____	Intellect	_____
_____	Emotions	_____
_____	Spirituality	_____
_____	Social life	_____
_____	Material	_____
_____	Work	_____

How did this work for you? Was it easier to think of the good or the bad? Where might that tendency lead you? Did you find yourself drawn into writing the same answer for both the best and the worst possible futures? If so, you have a natural tendency toward the idealistic style because you believe that you have a strong grasp on the future.

Learning to See the Future

Tools	Techniques
Planners, palm pilots	Write study plans weeks in advance. Plan steps along the way to make them come true.
Career planning	Ride your current values into the future. Link your learning to where you want to go.
Astronomy calendar	Note what phase the moon will be in, positions of the planets, and meteor showers. Create predictions like these that involve when you will take information in and when you will pull it out again.
Science fiction	Take note of others' views of the future. Make up stories about your own future, and imagine how your learning will support that future.

Creativity Is the Future

We can all see into the future to some extent. For example, what will happen if you drop your pencil? What will happen sometimes clashes with the creative view of what might happen. Try making predictions about future events; start with simple situations and get more complex later. Note for yourself three possible futures: the possible, the probable, and the unknown. Make notes, and set a time to check your predictions – in the future. Check out

Forbes, Inc. for its predictions in the business world
Harper's Index, and ask yourself, "What will happen next?"
Megatrends 2000 by John Naisbitt, Avon Books, 1991
http://www.futurist.com

IDEALIST

"Here's what I think will happen next…"

"I Don't Know" The Story of Win Le

Win Le was a poor Chinese farmer who lived 250 years ago. He had a comfortable hut, a loving wife, a sturdy son, and a good horse for plowing his fields. One day, Win Le's horse ran off into the hills. His wife wept. "We will never get our fields planted now," she said. "We will starve." Win Le ate his bowl of rice and said, "I don't know."

The next day Win Le and his son were in the horse's traces pulling the plow in front of the wife. Suddenly, the three looked up to see their horse returning with three other steeds. Win Le's wife was overjoyed. "We will be rich!" she sang, "We can sell two of these fine horses and send our son to school." Win Le said, "I don't know." He corralled the three new horses and went back to plowing with his own.

While his son was trying to make friends with the new horses, one of them kicked and broke the son's leg. The wife was frantic. "Our son will be crippled for life! No one will take care of us in our old age. We will die in poverty and misery." Win Le went to fetch a doctor, saying, "I don't know." The next day, while the physician was setting the young man's leg, representatives of the emperor arrived. They were conscripting young men into the army. "This boy will be of no use to the emperor," the physician said. "He will be unable to walk for at least two months." So the emperor's men took the two largest horses and left. Win Le smiled at his little family. "I just don't know," he said. It's easy to see how the wife was an idealist. Was Win Le?

Future Perfect

Here is a terrific exercise for a study group or even a family. The game is called Perfect Future and is played in two rounds. Round one is internal vision. Each person considers one aspect of the group, such as achievement, communication, behavior, learning, or conflict, and how it will improve in the coming year. Round two is comparing and discussing the visions. First, write everyone's ideals on big pieces of paper (use pictures, too), and put them up around the school, home, or study area. People will unavoidably move toward the ideals. It's fun to see how similar and different people's views of the future can be. It's also interesting to discuss how the futures might be achieved. To keep the conversation friendly, ask a lot of "what-if" questions. For example, "What if you don't have the resources to achieve your vision?" or "What if we learned everything we needed to know in life in the next six months?"

Working toward a New Future

Remember your favorite fairy tale or nursery rhyme. Now, imagine what happens after "happily ever after." What happens to the swan who is used to living with ducks? What does the cow do after she jumps over the moon? As you study a subject, ask yourself where the subject itself is going. What new discoveries might be made in the future? How will those discoveries affect the subject? Will they negate your current learning? Will they provide greater insights?

ANALYST - STRUCTURE, ORDER AND SENSE

The Science of Analytical Thinking

Analysts offer so much order in this serendipitous world. While others may envision the future or decide what to do, describe the obvious or look for relationships, analytic thinkers are looking at the structure and composition of what we already have. Analytic thinking is predictable, orderly, and precise. Analysts write policy and procedure manuals. They are also the folks who read and follow those procedures. Analysts may be scorned by pragmatists for wasting time on the obvious; they may be avoided by the idealists for having no vision; they may even be derided by the synthesists for missing the forest for the trees. Yet analysts patiently take big, complex things apart and therefore make the complex world more understandable to us all.

Deconstruct Your Learning

Do you think like an analyst? If so, you will tend to organize your topic of study into a simple structure. We like to use the information pyramid, arranging information like this:

Top – The subject or title of the learning

Middle – The main categories or logical themes

Bottom – Facts, proofs, examples, and illustrations

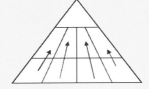

Taking notes in this form guarantees analytic thinking. Inductively, you see how the facts prove and illustrate the categories of information, which in turn substantiate the topic. Deductively, you show how the topic breaks logically into predictable parts, each of which must be substantiated by facts. If this makes sense to you, you have an analytical mind. If you do it in your head, you have a strong analytical mind. If it doesn't make sense, try doing it anyway. You will build your brain as you improve your many types of cognition.

Tools to Build an Analytical Memory

Tools	Techniques
Outlines, checklists	Break your large and complex learning into smaller parts.
Scorecards	List your learning topics and facts. Keep track of the ones you have learned.
Alpha files	List your learning in alphabetical order. The process of reviewing and sorting will help you remember more easily.
Tickler files	List the things you need to recall and when you need to recall them. Let the system do your remembering for you.
Maps, graphs, diagrams	Create an analytical color code that makes sense to you. Bring out important details; draw lines that link them to main categories and lines that link the main categories to the main subject.

ANALYST

"I want to take it apart and see how it works."

Creative Analysis

Analysis is frequently considered to be the antithesis of creativity. After all, analysis is taking things apart while creativity is building something new. But what if we combined the two? Take something apart, and then put the pieces back together differently.

In your learning, deconstruct two subjects using the pyramid on the left. Then mix and match the pieces to try to make interesting combinations that will help you retain the knowledge. For example: what chemistry was used at Waterloo? What philosophy might be used by mathematicians? What sports were played while the Beagle was visiting the Galapagos Islands? Also visit these sites.

http://www.2h.com – literally hundreds of personality tests
http://www.bizproweb.com – advice for business analysis
http://www.globalfindata.com/tbukcpi.htm – world finance

Kurt Can Do Many Things Well

Kurt has hundreds of interests and can talk intelligently about many, many things. He's not emotional, so in some ways he's not much fun.

But if you want to know about something and you want it explained well, call Kurt. This analyst is very well organized: he designed and built his own electric motor museum and catalogued every coil and brush. His kitchen has the shapes of pans and utensils painted on the wall, and every drawer is labeled and has compartments for all contents.

Kurt reads the labels of all the food he buys and patiently reads all the directions for the equipment he acquires. Go for a hike with Kurt and he'll tell you how many miles you've gone and how many miles there are to go. He can tell you the genus and specie of every plant in his yard. Kurt doesn't believe in God because, he says, "There is not enough factual proof."

Analyze Your Friends

Using the pyramid concept on the opposite page, select a particular learning point and assign different categories of the point to different members of the team. For example, you can ask one person to break down the economics, another to list the material components, a third to come up with the social implications, while a fourth lists the steps that made the learning point make sense.

As each person explains his or her analysis, everybody will develop a more thorough understanding of the whole.

A humorous variation of the game is to break the learning down to absurd levels; in learning a piece of software, add more levels to the bottom of the pyramid until you get down to the level of discovering the 1's and 0's in the bytes. How many levels down can you go?

Quick and Easy Pyramid Power

Grab a piece of paper. Take about five minutes to dissect this book in your mind using the information pyramid on the opposite page. The topic is Superfast Learning. What categories do you remember? Beneath each category, write your favorite exercises, ideas and stories.

Try this same exercise with any learning subject. Most people find that when the information is linked this way, they really know more than they thought they did.

YOUR EASY GENIUS ENVIRONMENT

Your Learning Environment

By now you have probably made three or four changes to your regular way of learning. We hope you are having more fun learning and are noticing real changes in the speed at which your mind integrates new information and makes it available for your body to use. Use this page to design your own perfect learning environment.

Here and Now

When you walk into your learning area, the first step is to get into a mental state of the here and now. You need to let go of everything in the outside world that does not help you to learn. You might try

- taking three deep breaths
- singing a song
- meditating for fifteen minutes
- doing a quick set of exercises
- looking in a mirror
- contemplating a peaceful picture

Reflection

Reflect for a time on your best learning modalities and intelligences. What are the influences (e.g., psychological, social, physiological) that best help you to learn?

How will you use them today to help you learn?

What Sounds Good for *You*

Don't forget about sounds. Do what you can in your learning environment to include the sounds that help you learn, such as

- nice music
- white noise generators for rain and wind sounds, or even soft static on the radio
- conversation
- silence

What works for you?

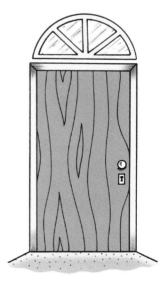

Your Place

In your environment, you can create different spaces, such as

- a place to read
- places to think
- areas for writing
- a snoozing zone

Your Visual Environment

What about things to look at? Set up your learning environment to include

- pictures or objects that inspire you
- uplifting graphs to measure your progress
- photos of people who matter to you
- colors that are conducive to learning

What works for you?

There Is More to Life

Learning is important, yet it is only one part of life. When you are not learning, where do you go and what do you do to

- reinvigorate yourself? _____
- be accepted? _____
- rest yourself? _____
- gain inspiration? _____
- feel challenged? _____
- connect with others? _____

Try to live way that supports your short- and long-term goals.

What picture might represent or remind you of your perfect place to learn with ease, security, and joy?

For reminders, check back to the appropriate section.

Your

Olfactory Environment

What can you smell that can help your learning?

Your Tactile Environment

Some people find it useful to touch things as they learn. I love the feel of a binder that snaps closed smoothly and securely. How about

- pens and pencils
- fabrics
- leather-bound books

Your Gustatory Environment

Your sense of taste is always with you. What would help you in your perfect learning environment?

BIBLIOGRAPHY

Adams, Scott; The Dilbert Future Harper Business New York, 1998

Alexander, F.M.; The Resurrection of the Body Delta Publishing New York 1971

Armstrong, Thomas; 7 Kinds of Smart, Plume, New York 1999

Armstrong, William H.; Study Tips: How to Study Effectively and Get Better Grades Barron's Educational Series, New York 1975

Barth, F. Diane, M.S.W.; Daydreams: Unlock the Creative Power of Your Mind Viking Books, New York 1997

Bear, Mark F. et al; Neuroscience: Exploring the Brain Williams and Wilkins, Baltimore 1996

Berg, Howard Stephen; Super Reading Secrets Warner Books Edition, New York 1992

Brodie, Richard; Virus of the Mind Integral Press, Seattle, 1996

Buber, Martin; I and Thou Charles Scribners and Sons, New York 1970

Canfield, Jack; Hansen, Mark Victor; Hewitt, Les; The power of Focus Health Communications, Deerfield Beach, FL 2000

Chevalier, Jean and Buchanan-Brown; The Penguin Dictionary of Symbols Penguin Books, London 1965

Claxton, Guy; Hare Brain Tortoise Mind The Ecco Press, New York 2000

Csikszenthihalyi, Mihaly; Creativity Harper Collins, New York 1996

Csikszenthihalyi, Mihaly; Flow Harper Perennial, New York 1990

DeBono, Edward; The Six Thinking Hats Little Brown & Co, New York 1999

Ibid; Lateral Thinking Perennial Library (Harper and Row), New York 1990

Dunbar, Robin; Grooming, Gossip and the Evolution of Language Harvard University Press, Cambridge 1997

Fritz Robert; The Path of Least Resistance: Learning to Become the Creative Force in Your Own Life Fawcett Columbine, New York 1984

Gardner, Howard; Multiple Intelligences: The Theory in Practice Basic Books, New York 1993

Gelb, Michael J.; Body Learning Owl Books, New York 1994

Gelb, Michael J.; How to Think Like Leonardo da Vinci Dell Trade Paperback, New York 1998

Green, Cynthia R. Ph.D.; Total Memory Workout Bantam Books, New York 1999

Gibbs, Jeann; Tribes: A New Way of Learning and Being Together Center Source Systems, Sausalito, CA 2000

Cunningham, Antonia, Ed.; Guinness Book of World Records Bantam Books, New York 2002

Gwaine Shackti; Creative Visualization Bantam New Age, New York 1985

Halpern, Steven; "Tools for Transformation" in New Realities Summer 1985

Hannaford, Carla, PhD.; Smart Moves Great Ocean Publishers, Atlanta 1995

Harman, Willis, Ph.D. and Rheingold, Howard; Higher Creativity Jeremy P. Tarcher (Putnam), New York 1984

Hegarty, Christopher; How to Manage Your Boss Ballentine Books, New York, 1982

Helmstetter, Shad, Ph.D.; What to Say When You Talk to Yourself Pocket Books, New York 1986

Hill, Napoleon; Think and Grow Rich Fawcett Books (Ballentine), New York 1990

Hobson, J. Allen; The Dreaming Brain Basic Books, New York 1988

Houston, Jean; The Possible Human Jeremy P. Tarcher (Putnam), Los Angeles 1982

Howard, Pierce J.; The Owner's Manual for the Brain Bard Press, Austin 2000

Jones, Patricia; Say It and Live It Currency Doubleday, New York 1954

Joudry, Peter; Sound Therapy St. Denis Publishers, Saskatchewan, 1984

Kagan, Spencer and Michael; Multiple Intelligences Kagan Cooperative Learning, San Clemente, CA 1998

Klein, Allen; The Healing Power of Humor Jeremy P. Tarcher (Putnam), Los Angeles 1988

Knowles, Malcolm; The Adult Learner: A Neglected Species Gulf Publishing, Houston 1978

Laborde, Genie Z.; Influencing with Integrity Syntony, Palo Alto, CA 1984

Ibid; Fine Tune Your Brain Syntony, Palo Alto, CA 1989

Lynch, Dudley; Strategy of the Dolphin Fawcett Books (Ballentine), New York 1988

Mann, Stanley A.C.S.W.; Triggers: A New Approach to Self-Motivation Prentice Hall, Englewood Cliffs, N.J. 1987

Bibliography, Continued

Masters, Robert, Ph.D. and Houston, Jean Ph.D.; Listening to the Body Delta, New York 1978

Mayer, Barbara; How to Succeed in High School VGM Career Horizons, San Antonio 1988

Michaud, Ellen; Boost Your Brain Power MJF Books, New York 1997

Ophiel; Art and Practice of Creative Visualization Samuel Weiser, York Beach, Maine 1997

Ostrander, Sheila; Super Memory; The Revolution Carroll & Graf Publishers, New York 1991

Pinker, Stephen; The Language Instinct Harper Perennial, New York 1994

Pierce, Howard J.; The Owner's Manual for The Brain Bard Press, 2000

Pritchett, Lou; Stop Paddling and Start Rocking the Boat Harper Collins, New York 1995

Reisberg, Daniel; Cognition: Exploring the Science of Mind W.W. Norton and Company, New York 1997

Robbins, Tony; The Giant Within Simon and Schuster, New York, 1985

Robbins, Tony; Unlimited Power Simon and Schuster, New York, 1986

Scannel, Edward E.; Even More Games Trainers Play McGraw Hill, New York 1994

Schrange, Michael; No More Teams: Mastering the Dynamics of Creative Collaboration Currency Doubleday, New York 1995

Schneider, Meir; Self Healing Routledge & Kegan Paul Ltd., London 1987

Sinetar, Marsha; The Mentor's Spirit St. Martin's Press / Griffin, New York 1998

Stein, Jean Marie; Super Brain Power Prentice Hall, New York 2000

Meltzer, M. (Ed); Thoreau: People, Principles and Politics Hill and Wang, New York 1963

Trudeau, Kevin; Kevin Trudeau's Mega Memory: How to Release Your Superpower Memory in 30 Minutes a Day Quill (Harper), New York 1997

VanOeck, Roger; A Kick in the Seat of the Pants Harper and Row, New York 1986

VanOeck, Roger; A Whack on the Side of the Head Harper And Row, New York 1986

Wenger, Win, Ph.D.; The Einstein Factor Pima Publishing, Boston 1996

Wurman, Richard S.; Information Anxiety Doubleday, New York 1989

Wycoff, Joyce; Mindmapping Berkeley Publishers Group, Berkeley, CA 1991

Zinker, Joseph; Creative Process in Gestalt Therapy Random House, New York 1977

WEBLIOGRAPHY

amcmusic.com
braingym.com
Catholic.org
chaordic.org
destinationimagination.org
draw3d.com
dustbunny.com/afk/
higherawareness.com
hti.umich.edu/k/koran/
kagan.com
kid-at-art.com
maledicta.org
newhorizons.org/trm_gardner.html
NLF.org
nols.edu/
primenet.com/~brendel/
reiinstitute.com
space.com
umc.org

Other interesting locations:

Ringling Brothers, Barnum and Bailey Clown College P.O.B. 1528 Venice FL 33595

CPSIA information can be obtained
at www.ICGtesting.com
Printed in the USA
LVIW021003081212

310664LV00002B